HOW TO TURN $ 5,000 INTO A MILLION

Heikin Ashi Trader

DAO PRESS

Copyright © 2019 by Heikin Ashi Trader

All rights reserved. No part of this book may be reproduced or utilized in any form or by any means, electronic or mechanical, including photocopying, recording, or by any information storage and retrieval system, without written permission of the publisher.

First edition, June 2019

The information presented herein represents the view of the author as of the date of publication. This book is presented for informational and entertainment purposes only. Due to the rate at which economic and cultural conditions change, the author reserves the right to alter and update his opinions based on new conditions. While every attempt has been made to verify the information in this book, neither the author nor his affiliates/partners assume any responsibility for errors, inaccuracies, or omissions. At no time shall the information contained herein be constructed as professional, investment, tax, accounting, legal or medical advice. This book does not constitute a recommendation or a warrant of suitability for any particular business, industry, website, security, portfolio of securities, transaction, or investment strategy.

Published by:
Dao Press
Dao Press is an imprint of Splendid Island, Ltd.
The Townhouse, 114-116 Fore Street #2
UK-Hertford, SG14 1AJ
All Rights Reserved

Table of Contents

Chapter 1: Can You Become A Millionaire On The Stock Market?...5

Chapter 2: Trade with the market's money, not with your own!..9

Chapter 3: Learning from the Grand Master of Speculators..17

Chapter 4: Scaling in – Scaling out 25

Chapter 5: Should You Use Stops? 38

Chapter 6: What do you do if the market is going in the wrong direction?..................................43

Chapter 7: Go Global Macro 47

Chapter 8: Look at the "Big Picture" 51

Chapter 9: Look for a catalyst................................58

Chapter 10: Mistakes to Learn From 69

Chapter 11: Success with cotton.............................75

Chapter 12: My ruble trade....................................81

Chapter 13: Thanks to Presidents Erdogan and Trump!..90

Chapter 14: Speculating with stocks.......................97

Chapter 15: Trade what you see 103

Chapter 16: How and When Should You Buy?..... 107

Chapter 17: Speculation is easier than day trading .. 111

Chapter 18: A separate account for each speculation.. 114

Chapter 19: With which financial instruments should I trade? 117

Chapter 20: Maximum risk and Margin Call 121

Chapter 21: Keep your trades to yourself 123

Chapter 22: On the way to the first million 128

Chapter 23: The Final Goal: Financial Freedom... 132

Addendum 1: Past financial crises......................... 138

Addendum 2: Useful websites 141

Glossary... 142

Other Books by Heikin Ashi Trader 150

About the Author 160

Chapter 1
Can You Become A Millionaire On The Stock Market?

Without a doubt, every trader is interested in the question of how to trade a small *account* up. How do you manage to increase this (usually small) seed capital? Or better still, how do you manage to make a small fortune out of this small sum? Preferably as fast as possible?

As soon as the money is in the brokerage account, most traders usually start looking for some kind of *holy grail method*, which sometimes takes years (as long as there is still money left). I would like to point out my view of things in this book – it will probably surprise some and will certainly upset others, because, what I have to say on the subject may not suit everyone.

Those who have read my other books know that I am critical of the idea of making a fortune out of a small capital investment. Yes, there are traders who succeeded in doing this. But they are few and far between. And above all, there are very few who have done so with the traditional short-term methods.

The goal of USD 1 million is a very high goal for most traders. In fact, some would say that one million is the sum you should bring with you when you go to the stock market. As the reader, you possibly know that even this kind of money is no guarantee that you will be successful. Most traders do not have so much capital when they start, anyway.

So the question is quite legitimate: Once you have made the decision that the stock market is the best way (I know someone who made his first million selling ice cream), what do you need to do if you want to earn a million?.

Big goals need big perspectives. If you plan to earn USD 500 with trading, then you need a different perspective than if your goal is USD 1 million. This book is about how to adopt such a perspective.

Unfortunately, many traders try to reach this goal by sticking to the USD 500 perspective. "I just need to reach this "modest goal" for enough days in a row," they say, "then I'll get to the million on my own. Sooner or later."

As a rule, these traders never reach their goal, and I firmly believe that the reason for this failure lies in their incorrect perspective. It is like looking for 5-cent pieces on the street. No doubt you could become a millionaire by collecting 5-cent pieces, but, in my opinion, that would take much too long.

Incidentally, I only came to understand this simple truth gradually. I was one of those traders who looked for 5 cents every day. The tragedy of this approach is that, every now and then, you actually will find a few 5-cent pieces. That little surge of happiness that one feels, makes one think one is on the right track. No doubt, the person who collects 5-cent pieces will reach his million, one day. For example, if he finds one of those coins every day, he simply needs to repeat this success for the next 20 million days. I think the reader will see the absurdity of this idea.

So, if you set yourself a high goal, you should look for ideas that will get you to your destination a little faster than our brave collector of 5-cent pieces. In this book, we will look at how one can find such opportunities and what perspective we need to adopt (rather than walking around with our eyes glued to the sidewalk).

I would like to present the reader with a strategy that, in my opinion, makes it possible to make a fortune on the stock market. I am not saying that this is the only way, because there are thousands of ways to make money on the stock market. But it is a radical method, because it assumes that, under normal circumstances, the trader with a small starting capital will not be able to achieve this. Nevertheless, the possibility exists to make a fortune on the stock market with just a small investment, by procuring the missing capital from another source, outside of yourself. The strategy that I present here starts with the assumption that the trader cannot achieve this with *his* money but only *with the market's money*. He will have to learn to get the money from where it is. And he'll have to do it with chutzpah. In other words, he will have to take serious risks. I think that speaks for itself. To say anything else would be a lie.

Just as it is possible to build a real estate empire without a dollar of equity, so it is possible to build a large trading account within a relatively short time with a small starting capital (USD 5000 or even less). I am contradicting myself here, because I have already said, in previous books, that this is not possible. What I meant was that it is not possible to do so with conventional trading methods. In other words, you will have to go very unconventional ways if you want to achieve that goal.

Chapter 2

Trade with the market's money, not with your own!

My best year of trading was 2008. But most of the money I got did not come from my day trading or scalping. Although those methods also worked well that year, most of my profits came from <u>a single trade</u>. *A single!* I earned more with that trade than I had in the previous three years. This experience was a kind of breakthrough for me. These are the kinds of moments when you discover completely new possibilities. That was the case with the one trade with which I made a six-figure sum. It was the time of the financial crisis. Lehman Brothers was broke. The stock markets had plummeted. Almost everyone was sitting on big losses, while I was able to reap the biggest profit of my trader career, because *I was standing on the other side*. No, I was not short in stocks, even though that would have been an excellent idea. I was long in silver. That was my only position at that exciting time: long silver.

I was convinced, that in a crisis of confidence of this magnitude (subprime crisis), it would be a good idea to buy a so-called "crisis currency". Investors like to park their money in markets that are considered safe havens in times of turmoil. Traditionally, these are the precious metals, especially gold and silver of course, but also currencies of certain countries, such as the Swiss franc or the Norwegian krone. At the time, I did not understand that this also included the US dollar. Escaping the risk usually helps the markets that are considered relatively stable or "low risk". I chose silver because I assumed silver would outperform gold in this crisis. This assumption turned out to be correct, but unfortunately, it did not really materialize until three years later, when silver climbed to stratospheric heights in the wake of the Euro crisis.

Still, my silver trade of 2008 was a success, though the movement on silver in early 2008 was modest compared to what happened in 2010-2011. I started building smaller positions in the range of around USD 13 or USD 14, during the subprime crisis in late 2017. These first positions turned to profits, quickly and easily. After a few days, I already had a book profit of over USD 1000. Not bad, you might think, and under normal circumstances I would have been happy with that gain, and I would have sold the position.

Incidentally, I did not intend to keep that trade going for long. I gladly admit that the trade was intended as a day trade. Once the position had gained nicely, I thought: why not keep it going a little longer and try to get more out of the trade? And indeed, silver rose the next day, and I had the courage to buy another contract. But you have to be aware of the hysteria of those days. The media was full of bad news, not to say catastrophic news. The stock markets plummeted worldwide. And when the news of the Lehman Brothers bankruptcy on the ticker came on September 15, the dam broke. The crisis was complete!

My silver trade, on the other hand, did very well. The more the silver price rose, the more contracts I bought. A few days later, I already had five-digit profits. But, if you are now thinking that such a profit would lift you to a permanent state of elation, you are mistaken. Prices do not go straight up (I wish they would). Not at all. When markets go wild and volatility picks up, prices fluctuate so much that they can go just as wildly the other direction. I remember that my silver position was USD 17,000 in profits one morning, and only USD 12,000 in the afternoon, due to a correction. A book loss of USD 5000 in just a couple of hours!

That was much more than I would allow myself under normal conditions. But you have to be able to live with that if you want to increase your position systematically. Let me point out that I did not have a smartphone at the time (I'm a bit old-fashioned). Having a number of contracts in a trend market is a disconcerting thing (actually, great success is also somewhat disconcerting, which is why most people prefer to live without it). So I had to open my laptop every time, to see what was happening to my silver position.

At the beginning of January 2008, silver struck a resistance of about USD 15. This resistance had lasted for two years. I had placed several stop buy orders above this level, all of which were executed when the outbreak came. Soon I had doubled my position again. Now it became really exciting. The fluctuations in my account were now quite wild. Within a minute I was several hundred dollars richer or poorer, and soon it was to be thousands of dollars ...

Image 1: Silver, Monthly Chart 2006 - 2019

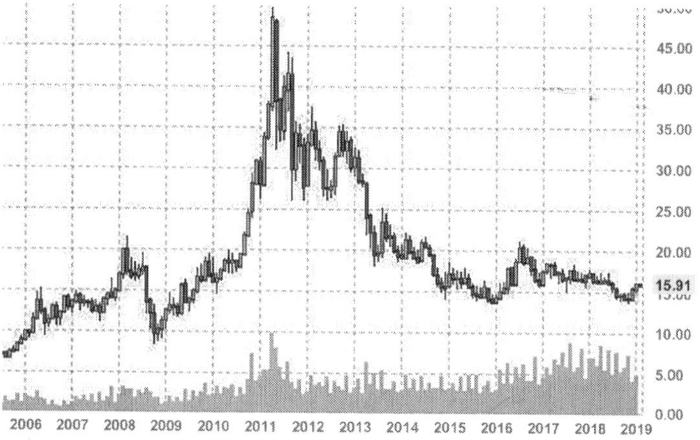

I remember well that I felt I was on the safe side with this position. I knew that I had a winner and that all I had to do was rigorously trade the upward movement in silver. This was an extraordinary situation, because I had only a few thousand euros in my brokerage account. I used it to experiment and perform occasional swing trades, if I saw an opportunity. If I remember correctly, I had about EUR 2,700 in that account. Not much, considering that, thanks to this one silver trade, I eventually had a book profit of more than EUR 40,000. So, within a few weeks, I had made more than 1,000% profit, thanks to the leverage I used, and the fact that I traded with the money that was on the market. That was the whole secret of this trade. I did not trade with my own money. <u>I traded with the market's money.</u>

I suggest that we take a closer look at this, because some readers might not understand what I am saying. If you buy a property and finance 70% of it, you are basically not buying this object with your money, but with the bank's money. The bank pays for the major part of this property, because it considers the property as collateral, and the house remains the property of the bank until the last installment has been paid.

Something similar happens in the stock market, once you have book profits. As long as you do not realize these book profits (you do not sell your position), that money does not belong to you, but to the broker. However, this book profit allows you to buy additional contracts, because they will be credited to you through the daily settlement. So, this book profit allows you to buy a larger position than you would normally have been able to buy with your small capital. This is a comparable leverage – as if you were buying a property with a loan from the bank.

And, of course, you cannot call your accumulated book profit your own until you sell your position and earn the profit. But, as long as you do not sell, you can continue to buy, provided you are still right in terms of the market direction, and the trend continues to grow in your favor.

This approach is very different from closing your position every day and reopening it the next morning (which is what a day trader does, for example). At first glance, day trading seems less risky, but it is easy to forget that, every day, the trader carries the whole the risk. He risks *his* money every day. His *own* capital is fully at risk.

However, if you do as I did on the silver market in 2008, at some point, you will no longer be risking your own money – you will begin to speculate with the market's money (thanks to your book profits). Technically, you may not see the difference, but in terms of risk management, the difference is huge. As soon as your first purchased contracts run into profit and your book profit increases, you have a "free trade", so to speak. From that moment on, you can use your book profits to expand your position. So you do not buy with your own money but with the market's money (or with the bank's money, if you will). Moreover, I think that you should not keep the leverage on your position too small when you find yourself in this comfortable situation – quite the contrary. From now on, you should really grab the ball and expand your position seriously, because that is the only way you can make real financial progress.

The same is true for the clever real estate investor. He does not buy his properties with his own money. He buys them with the bank's money. And the more properties he owns, the more he buys. It is a proven concept. If you research a little, you'll find that, apart from those who have built a successful business, most rich people have become wealthy with real estate.

Over the course of January and February that year, silver rose to over USD 20. While it was on its way to the top, I bought more contracts. In the end, not as aggressively as in the beginning, because, after studying the chart, I had the feeling that, at some point, silver was going to reach a peak, and then the inevitable correction would occur. This feeling was soon to come true. In March, silver reached its high. The volatility was almost insane. I started selling my contracts and locking in my profits. In hindsight, I sold a bit too late and lost out on some of the profit I could have made. But in hindsight you are always smarter. The trade was a big success, and I was able to live on that kind of money for a long time.

After I had closed the position completely, I did not do anything for months. It took time for me to recover from my own success. Anyone who believes that success is something great and simple is wrong. It is really scary, because you are confronted with something that is unknown in you. Something that is much bigger and more powerful than you.

Chapter 3
Learning from the Grand Master of Speculators

In stumbling into this trade by chance, I unconsciously did something that would only become a real method in years to come. Of course, I knew what I was doing. I had heard of other traders who had completed these types of trades successfully. And of course there are examples of traders in trading literature who have become wealthy in this way. But, let's be honest! You can only really understand a method if you apply it yourself. Theoretical knowledge does not help you at all. Since I did not intend to do such a trade, I was not prepared for the potential risks of this method. Neither did I know what I would go through emotionally during the time I was holding that position.

In retrospect, I took time to study the traders who had used this strategy successfully, and above all, of course, the American trader and speculator Jesse Livermore. He is probably the most prominent example of a trader who went the whole hog. You can read about Jesse Livermore on the Internet, and of course I also recommend the book by Edwin Lefevre "Reminiscences of a Stock Operator". It describes the method we are talking about here, in an entertaining way.

Of course Livermore did not master his method from the beginning. He started off playing the market in the short term, like most of us (times do not change). At some point he realized that the big money could only be earned with the big market movements. Of course, for this, he needed a different method to that of a day trader. First, one has to say that Livermore traded primarily in equities. There was no such thing as trading with an index at the time. However, you can apply this method perfectly in the usual trading markets such as SP500, Nasdaq, Dax, IBEX, CAC40 or EUR/USD.

Before Livermore became active at all, he observed the markets. This is the first pillar of his method. Livermore was a good observer. Above all, he looked at the market leaders of that time, the driving forces of the stock markets. He studied the most important stocks of the sectors. In his time, these were, for example, Bethlehem Steel or Northern Pacific. Of course, today those would be stocks like Apple, Google, Amazon or Facebook. He watched the behavior of those leaders. He looked at how they responded to certain news, whether they recovered quickly from a negative news announcement (bullish) or not (bearish). If you want to get involved with Livermore's method, you can refer to the little book by Richard D. Wyckoff "Jesse Livermore's Methods of Trading in Stocks".

In my opinion, the key word here is "observing". In other words, Livermore may have had no position in the market for weeks or even months. He was 100% in cash during those periods. That is not easy for many traders, because you have the feeling that if you have no position at all, you are not involved in the stock market, and you could miss out on good opportunities. Nothing could be farther from the truth. 100% cash is a position. Actually, it is a very important position.

Before you can act, you first have to learn to observe closely and wait for the really good opportunities to come your way. Patience is one of the most important virtues that you will need to develop, if you want to be successful with this method. It is undoubtedly the hardest part of the method. You will have to learn to transfer money to a brokerage account and then do nothing, for weeks, sometimes even for months.

Can you do this, even if your broker bombards you with emails, and asks you to start trading because his systems are sending him great "signals". Again, you will have to learn from Livermore, who hated nothing more than the so-called tips that you get from everywhere as soon as you enter the stock market. He tried to free himself from these confusing influences by all the means he had at his disposal. He did this by partially isolating himself from the outside world, so that he was only able to listen to his own intuition and instincts. He did not become active until he saw a real opportunity, <u>coming from his own observations</u>.

I think that this habit is much more difficult to learn today, than it was in Livermore's day. Today, the news, opinions and tips, and whatever distractions the broker industry may invent – do not only come in the form of newspapers, magazines, newsletters, emails and alerts. They also flash at you at the most inopportune moments, on the small, flat device that each of us carries around permanently, wherever we go.

You must learn to forget about all that noise and disregard all the supposedly interesting stock market pages and the seemingly interesting articles by analysts. Or even better, do not even read them anymore. You must learn to become <u>a completely independent observer</u>, and a completely independent-minded person.

If you have acquired this important capacity of being able to ignore what others are saying, you will one day begin <u>to perceive signals from the market yourself</u>. This is very important, because you cannot trade this method if you cannot observe and think own, and have therefore have not formed opinion of the market. Did I just say that get your own opinion of the market? Yes, even though you may have read everywhere, that you can only be a good trader if you have no opinion of the market! This may apply to short-term strategies such as day trading, but it does not apply if you want to make a trade, as I did with silver in 2008. At the end of 2007, due to the financial crisis, I was bullish on gold and silver and the market proved me right.

Will you always be right regarding the direction of the market? By no means! You will experience, again and again, that you have to close your first position at a loss or that your position does not progress at all. You will experience that the market does not confirm your opinion. There is nothing wrong with that. That's part of the game. Hopefully, you will get out of it with a small loss and return to the observation status. For weeks or even months. After all, you want to respect the first law of a trader: preserve your trading capital.

Second, you also have to maintain another, even more important asset, and I do not mean the amount of money in your brokerage account. Your most important asset is <u>your ability to think and observe independently</u>. As long as you have a position (and our money is exposed to market risks), you cannot think anymore. You are emotionally involved with the trade, and the bigger the position becomes, and the more money there is in the game, the more you will battle with your feelings and emotions.

If your emotions are so strong that you can hardly bear it, then your position is probably too big. If your emotions are so weak that you hardly feel them, then it is probably too small and you should add to your position. It goes both ways. For example, I was one who tended to keep my positions too small. Therefore, my silver trade was a sort of cathartic moment for me, because it forced me to give it a go when the opportunity presented itself.

One has to realize that making money on the stock market does not happen in the same way as it does in the usual professions. With a regular job, you get the same amount each month. That gives those who walk this path a sense of security. There is no such thing on the stock market. Oh well! Some think that it is possible. Day trading, for example, is an attempt to reintroduce the security of an office job, with regular income coming through the back door.

On the stock market, there are only asymmetric earnings. What does that mean? Mostly, you do not earn anything, or you could even lose a bit. And then comes the day when the roast is served. These are the occasional opportunities where you can make a small fortune. Needless to say, these opportunities are only available to the trader who is prepared. And that is why it is so important to build your own independent observation post, as Jesse Livermore did.

Then, if you see an opportunity based on *your* observations, you should buy (or sell if you go short)

a small first position. This first position is <u>to test the water</u>. But the first position also has another important function. According to Livermore, you cannot judge a market until you are in it yourself. This first little position tells you whether or not you are in the right market. If you do not have a position, there is no way of knowing. You have to be emotionally involved with your own money.

If the trade feels good and the market is moving in the right direction, you can start buying more contracts (or more shares if you trade in stocks). Of course, you will not catch a major trend every time, as I did with my silver trade. Sometimes you will have to interrupt the trade, because the trend does not continue or even turns in the other direction. But if you follow the criteria that I will explain in the following chapters, you will occasionally make a nice profit.

Chapter 4
Scaling in – Scaling out

The real secret of a successful trading business is not the perfect entry or the perfect exit from a position. Too many traders put too much emphasis on this aspect of a strategy. <u>The real secret is ensuring that your winners are infinitely bigger than your losers.</u>

If you have a book profit with a trade, you should not frantically sell and pocket the profits, as many traders do. You should see this book gain as an opportunity or an option. You should ask yourself whether or not there is still a lot to gain here. So, the right strategy is to invest in this book profit.

In principle, this trading technique can be carried out with any financial instrument. Of course, you will benefit most if you build such positions with leveraged instruments, such as futures or options. You will learn to reinvest your unrealized gains on open trades. Put simply: You only buy additional contracts (or stocks) when the previous ones are already in profit. In this way you can build up large positions in a market

without increasing the initial risk of the position. The RRR (Risk Reward Ratio) will gradually improve in this way.

However, if you do the opposite, averaging down, you increase your risk. Averaging down when prices fall further only makes sense for long-term oriented investors who, for example, have a dividend strategy.

Right from the beginning I would like to make it clear that the technique of buying up is easy to understand, but it is not necessarily easy to carry out. This technique goes against the "nature" of the trader. As soon as a trade becomes profitable, the trader wants to hedge it through active stop management, or even pocket the gains. The trader must therefore muster a good deal of self-control and discipline, in order not to concede to his natural tendency to take the first profits and run. On the contrary. Instead of taking the profits and getting out of the market, he has to learn to buy additional contracts (or shares). He has to learn to increase his position when the starting position is in profit. This requires courage, but also the insight to understand that this is the only way to reach substantial profits.

The method that I present here is not the same as so-called pyramiding. It is important to clearly describe the difference. Building a pyramid in a market means that the first position you buy is the largest (the base of the pyramid). Each additional position you buy should be a bit smaller than the previous one, usually half the size. So if you start with 100 shares, then the second position should only be 50 shares, the third 25 and so on.

The idea of this approach is clear. A trader who works with this methodology believes that the longer a trend lasts, the bigger the likelihood is, that it will turn. That's why he reduces the risk. Although I can understand the logic of this methodology, it is a suboptimal idea for me. If you are right about your market assessment and the trend continues, then you should definitely go for it. Because, if you are already sitting on good profits, you can, as already mentioned, speculate with the market's money.

You should internalize this difference. Risk is not equal to risk. If you are a day trader and close your positions every night, you start afresh every morning. This means that you risk YOUR money every day. In that sense, one could say that day trading is suboptimal in terms of risk management. Every day, you risk YOUR money in the markets.

By contrast, if you scale into a trend, you only risk your money with the first position. For the second contract you pay with the market's money (with the book profits from the first position). Therefore, I am not talking about pyramiding, but about **scaling in – scaling out**.

Unlike building a pyramid, you cannot increase your position until the first position has enough book profit, so that this book gain enables you to buy a second position. This second position is not smaller than the first – it is usually the same size. For example, if you trade futures, the smallest unit is 1 contract. You cannot reduce or divide this unit.

In that sense, you double your position with the purchase of a second contract. If this one also runs into profit, the book profits of the first two contracts allow you to buy a third contract. From now on, you do not double your position, as you did with the second contract – your position increases by 33%. The longer the trend lasts, and the more contracts you can buy, and the smaller your risk will be, even though you substantially increase your position with each new purchase. Thus, with each new contract you buy, you greatly increase the chance of a huge win, while minimizing your risk, thanks to accumulated book profits.

Therefore, in my view, scaling in – scaling out is a much less risky method than day trading or even holding a stock portfolio that you have bought 100% with your own funds. I hope the difference is clear.

An intelligent investor tries to generate a maximum return with the lowest possible initial risk. This is the case with real estate (here the bank finances your property and your tenant pays the installments). And this is how it should be when you buy a company or company shares (through private placements, not by buying shares in the market).

In my opinion, the method of scaling in – scaling out therefore belongs in an advanced investor's toolbox.

The first position is nothing more than a hypothesis, and this is really how you should see it. You make an assumption as to how a market might develop (from the moment of purchase or sale on a short sale). This assumption is either confirmed or not. Basically, the output does not matter. Sometimes you'll be right, sometimes wrong.

That's why you should not pyramid (buy the largest position at the beginning), because you then buy the biggest position with *your* money. It is better to buy the larger portion of the position with the market's money (through book profits).

Of course, the scaling in – scaling out method is not completely risk-free, because a medium or small reversal can reduce or even destroy the accrued book profit. Needless to say, if this happens, you should start to reduce your position and close it completely if necessary. Then it is a case of "nothing ventured, nothing gained".

Ideally, you should build a position in such a market, so that this never happens. That's why I recommend that you do not use this method on medium trends (which take a few days) or even on short-term trends (a few hours). That's the common mistake many make. This method is designed for the major stock market trends. The idea is that you are in the trade for a matter of weeks, and possibly several months. Only in this way you can achieve above-average profits, even with a small starting capital. This is hardly possible with trends that only last a few days. The position takes time to develop.

For example, if you buy a stock at USD 20, your goal should not be to sell it at USD 22. That's not a big trend. But if you hold onto the stock for six months, and it rises to USD 35, then you have the time to build a significant position with it, which you finance with book profits.

Scaling in and scaling out is not unusual, by the way. It is a common method used by many traders, and also hedge funds, to build significant positions in a market. However, if you have no previous experience with this method, I recommend that you start with a calm approach and do not buy too many contracts on the first trade. I will demonstrate how the technique works with two examples.

Image 2: Crude Oil: Scaling in – Scaling out

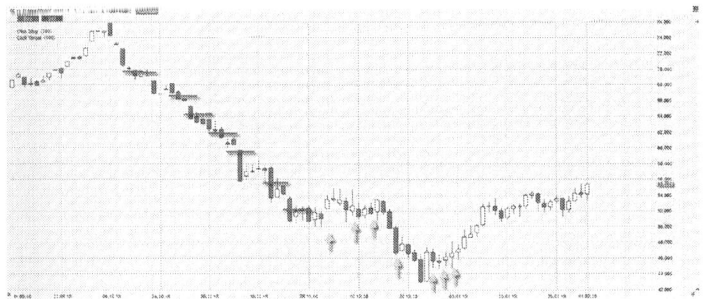

As an example, let us have a closer look at this short trade in the crude oil futures. After the market gave a bearish signal, the trader went short with a first futures contract at USD 69.70 (small red line in the upper left corner of the chart). As the market continued to fall, he sold at USD 66.40, a second contract short. Overall, he sold seven contracts in this falling market. When crude oil hit the USD 50 mark in late November 2018, the future started to go sideways at that level. After not falling any further for a week, the trader was aware that a reversal or correction could happen, and started scaling out. He bought back a first contract on the market (first green arrow on the bottom left). Thus, he was only six contracts short and had realized the profit of one contract. When the market stabilized above USD 50 after three days, he closed a second contract and a third contract two days later, so that he was only four contracts short.

The trader was rewarded for his patience because on December 17, Crude Oil fell below USD 50. When the futures fell below USD 47 the day after, he closed a fourth contract. Now he was only three contracts short. The low of this move was USD 42.72. Of course, the trader could not predict this low. As the future began to rise again in the following days, he gradually closed the three remaining contracts (green arrows on the right).

Although the trader did not reach the optimum in this example, he nevertheless made a successful trade. He was in this move with seven contracts short, all of which he was able to close at a profit. Overall, the trader was in the position from October 18, 2018 to January 2, 2019 – almost two and a half months. This is a typical time frame for the type of position trade we are talking about here.

Therefore, we are going to take a closer look at the trade and the development of the individual contracts. In this case the trader traded the crude oil futures contract at the CME (code CL). The tick size (smallest price fluctuation) is USD 0.01 per barrel. The value of a tick is USD 10.0. The overnight margin of his American broker was USD 2,145. This means that the trader needed to have at least USD 2,145 in the account, in order to trade a contract. However, he was able to go short with further contracts, thanks to the book profit of the first contracts.

Contract 1: Short USD 69.70, flat USD 53.50, profit: 1,620 tics x USD 10 = USD 16,200

Contract 2: Short USD 66.40, flat USD 54.05, profit: 1,235 tics x USD 10 = USD 12,350

Contract 3: Short USD 64.20, flat USD 52.10, profit: 1,210 tics x USD 10 = USD 12,100

Contract 4: Short USD 61.90, flat USD 46.60, profit: 1,530 tics x USD 10 = USD 15,300

Contract 5: Short USD 59.70, flat USD 45.90, profit: 1,380 tics x USD 10 = USD 13,800

Contract 6: Short USD 55.80, flat USD 46.10, profit: 970 tics x USD 10 = USD 9,700

Contract 7: Short USD 52.20, flat USD 47.50, profit: 470 tics x USD 10 = USD 4,700

Total: **8,415 tics x USD 10 = USD 84,150**

If the trader had gone short with only one contract, for example the first one, then his profit would have been USD 16,200. Certainly not bad, but I hope I could demonstrate the advantage of the scaling-in method in this example, where a profit of USD 84,150 was recorded. In other words, the trader was able to realize a profit of USD 84,150 with a bet of USD 2,140 (initial margin of the first contract). These are the trades I am talking about, and they really help to grow your account substantially (and in many cases, your financial position too). That's why, in my opinion, it's worth waiting patiently for such opportunities.

This example is a bit idealistic. Here, we were dealing with a market that was gradually going down, like a flight of stairs. Of course, this situation makes it easy for a trader to build a position step by step. He was also able to quietly scale out when the market reached the USD 50 level. Normally, you would expect a proper reversal here, which forces the trader to close his positions quickly. Since this was not the case, the trader could benefit from another fall in the price of oil with the four remaining contracts.

It should be clear to the reader, that such an ideal case does not always occur. As a rule, if we are dealing with a real "crisis market", things are a bit more chaotic. The next example illustrates such a situation.

Image 3: Natural Gas Future, 4-hour chart

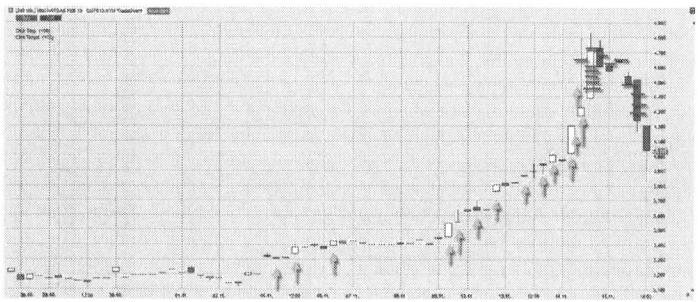

In the example in Image 3 the trader chose to trade the main contract on Natural Gas (NG), which is traded on the Nymex. His American broker required an overnight margin of USD 2,420 per contract. If he had traded with a European broker for example, he would have had to deposit USD 5,000 to trade even one contract. The smallest price fluctuation (tic) in this contract is 0.001. The value of a single tick is USD 10.

After the future on Natural Gas had fluctuated between USD 2.50 and USD 3.00 for months in 2018, the price suddenly jumped above USD 3.20 on November 5. This prompted the trader to open a first test position in this market (first green arrow at the bottom left). When the price rose to USD 3.40 the same day, the trader bought a second contract. On November 6, the futures rose above USD 3.40, so the trader bought a third contract. It took until November 9, before the trader could buy again. The market went sideways for several days.

From November 9 to 13, the trader was able to buy six additional contracts. He was now long by nine contracts. November 14 was the day when the future began to rise in a parabolic way. During the day, the future rose from USD 4.00 to over USD 4.80, an increase of 20%! As you can see, the trader bought four more contracts on the way up, but soon he had to start to scale out, due to the insane volatility. In the afternoon and late evening of November 14, the trader sold nine of his fourteen contracts. He closed the next five the next day, at less favorable prices. His assumption that the future would continue to rise the next day, maybe even over USD 5.00, had not materialized, so he had to sell the rest of his position.

Although the trader was far from selling at the high of this move in Natural Gas, he made a considerable profit. This trade only lasted 10 days, an unusually short period for this type of speculation. You see, the trader was able to buy more and more contracts on the way up, thanks to the book profits. Then, he had to scale out of his position relatively fast. In this case, within a few hours. It is important to take this into consideration when market volatility begins to increase disproportionately. In general, this is a sign that the movement is coming to an end. Let us take a closer look at the profits of the traded contracts here.

Contract 1: Long USD 3,200, flat USD 4,450, profit: 1,250 tics x USD 10 = USD 12,500

Contract 2: Long USD 3,400, flat USD 4,500, profit: 1,100 tics x USD 10 = USD 11,000

Contract 3: Long USD 3,430, flat USD 4,550, profit: 1,120 tics x USD 10 = USD 11,200

Contract 4: Long USD 3,550, flat USD 4,580, profit: 1,030 tics x USD 10 = USD 10,300

Contract 5: Long USD 3,600, flat USD 4,600, Profit: 1,000 tics x USD 10 = USD 10,000

Contract 6: Long USD 3,650, flat USD 4,650, Profit: 1,000 tics x USD 10 = USD 10,000

Contract 7: Long USD 3,800, flat USD 4,720, profit: 920 tics x USD 10 = USD 9,200

Contract 8: Long USD 3,870, flat USD 4,680, profit: 810 tics x USD 10 = USD 8,100

Contract 9: Long USD 3,950, flat USD 4,620, profit: 1,000 tics x USD 10 = USD 10,000

Contract 10: Long USD 4,000, flat USD 4,650, profit: 670 tics x USD 10 = USD 6,700

Contract 11: Long USD 4,100, flat USD 4,480, profit: 380 tics x USD 10 = USD 3,800

Contract 12: Long USD 4,200, USD 4,450 flat, Profit: 250 tics x USD 10 = USD 2,500

Contract 13: Long USD 4,300, flat USD 4,350, profit: 50 tics x USD 10 = USD 500

Contract 14: Long USD 4,450, flat USD 4,290, loss: 160 tics x USD 10 = - USD 1,600

Total: **10,420 tics** **USD 104,200**

As you can see, the trade was well worth it, even though the trader had to close one contract at a loss (contract 14). If you have to scale out fast, this can happen. It's important to keep in mind that prices may fluctuate wildly at the end of such a move. And although most of the profit is realized at the end, one should beware of the corrections or reversals that could then occur.

Chapter 5
Should You Use Stops?

The biggest advantage of the scaling in – scaling out technique is to be found in the reduction of the initial risk. The trader who always trades with the same position size takes the same risk again and again. However, if you build up your position gradually, you minimize the risk gradually too. At some point, it disappears completely. With the fourth or fifth contract, you will have built up so much book profit that you cannot lose anymore. While, of course, every time you buy a new contract, you will have a market risk for that specific contract, based on your trading capital, the accrued profit protects you from a new risk to your account. That's the fundamental difference that you should understand, and that's why this technique enables you far better risk management than you would have otherwise.

Of course, you always have to be aware of a scenario in which an established trend suddenly turns, and the market starts to move massively in the other direction. In that case, your contracts, which were profitable at first, suddenly start to lose. Depending on how many contracts (or shares) you currently hold, such a countermovement can quickly lead to significant losses. You will then receive margin calls from your broker. As soon as the first margin call comes in, you should not hesitate to start to scale out immediately. You may even need to close the full position, and you will then have to classify this speculation under the category "Failed Attempts".

Another way to reduce risk, when the market goes in the wrong direction, is to secure your positions with stops. Of course, if you've bought multiple contracts and you want to secure them all with stops, things will get a bit complicated. It is up to each trader whether he wants to use stops or not.

In fact, when you work with stops, you basically are not building a single position. Rather, you have many individual trades side by side. You split your position into many small trades. There is nothing wrong with that, and I recommend that traders do it that way first.

The question is, how you should do it, because no matter which stop method you use, you will inevitably experience that a short-term correction will put contracts out of the market if you put your stops too close to the entry level. Despite this disadvantage, I recommend that beginners work this way to start with. You must first become familiar with this method and gain confidence, so that, at a later stage, you can start to use more generous stops.

A beginner using this technique can pull the stop of the first contract, to break even, as soon as he buys the second contract. He should do the same thing with the second contract, as soon as he buys the third, and so on. In this way, his maximum risk is always equal to R1, or in other words, it is never bigger than his initial risk when he bought the first contract. This is a conservative approach, but it is clear and not open to any interpretation.

A second option would be to work with trailing stops, which you could set for every single contract on the way. This gives you a bit more flexibility, and it also gives you a better chance to get the maximum out of the trade, which is the big advantage of a trailing stop. Unfortunately, with this method, you will experience that contracts are put out of the market by reversals or counter movements, which of course is especially annoying if the trend continues thereafter.

Of course, if a reversal takes two or three contracts out of the market, you can always buy them back later, but I only recommend that traders who are already familiar with the method do this.

A more advanced method of risk management is to hedge the position. With this method, the trader takes the opposite trade at the same underlying basic value, or in a correlated instrument, in order to protect the account from major losses. As a rule, he should choose the same number of contracts that his position currently has. For example, if he is five contracts long in the EUR/USD currency pair, he will hedge his position with five short positions in the same market. Should the EUR/USD turn 180 degrees against his expectations, his stop-sell orders (short orders) will be executed gradually. Thus, he "freezes" his position, so to speak. In this way, the loss is limited. It results from the difference between the entry price of the long position and the entry price of the short position.

It is important to know that not every forex broker will allow you to hedge positions. Therefore, if you want to use hedging as a risk management tool, you should inquire with your broker in advance, as to whether this is possible.

Once the hedge has been built and the position is "frozen", the trader has several options. He can close the full position, including the hedge, and thus take the loss. In general, this is the best solution. But he can also make partial closures and trade with a reduced position, should the market give him indications that it will develop in the desired direction again.

Hedging is a complex topic, and experience has shown that it does not work for the majority of traders. For most traders, traditional stops are still the best solution. I see hedging more as a kind of "emergency brake", which only comes into force when the position is really in danger and bigger losses could occur. In my view, only traders who really know what they are doing, should use hedging to protect open positions.

Chapter 6
What do you do if the market is going in the wrong direction?

No matter how well you prepare your trades, you will experience, from time to time, that a position that you currently hold does not work out as desired. Perhaps it is not moving at all, and your test position changes from slightly in the plus to slightly in the minus. Of course, this is the easy version. You can either close the position, and wait until something really starts happening, or the second option, is to push the stop closer to your entry price, in the hope that the market will eventually begin to move properly. Usually, you will be stopped out. It is a well-known trader's wisdom, that positions that go into profit immediately, are usually the best. If they do not, always be careful.

On the other hand, if your position initially goes in the right direction, and you are already able to buy three or four contracts, and then the market suddenly turns 180 degrees, you should not panic. Emotions such as panic, are an unmistakable sign that, either your position is too big, or that this method does not suit you.

If the market goes against you for a few hours or days, and the losses become too big, instead of hurrying to close the whole position, you can close a part of your position. For example, you could sell the last two contracts you bought, that are now at a loss, and then watch the market until it turns back in your favor. The big advantage of multiple entries is that you do not need to close the whole position when things are not going well. If you only have one contract, it goes without saying, that you have to get out completely.

When you start working with the scaling in – scaling out method, you will automatically learn <u>to become an active manager of your positions</u>. This technique is based on the insight that the ideal entry into a position does not usually happen. As a rule, you will need to be patient, and give your first position time to become profitable.

Incidentally, not all trend markets develop in a straight line, in one direction. That's why I recommend trading on higher time frames, such as daily charts or even weekly charts. If your position is showing a decent profit and you have four or five contracts in the market, then you do not necessarily have to sell when the market goes against you for a few days. Admittedly, this scenario causes stress for some traders, but you should be able to withstand it if you want to become a millionaire.

The only real risk is the loss of your initial capital. You should act when the first margin calls come in, at the latest.

As each market evolves differently, there can be no blueprint for building positions. It's up to you to decide whether your position is simply too big, or maybe too small. Your task, as the manager of your account, is <u>to generate the maximum return with the minimum risk</u>. If you only minimize your risks, and do not buy enough contracts if the trade is going well, you violate the second part of this rule. Then you behave like those traders who trade with a linear position management. The whole strength of the method I recommend here is to understand that stock market success has little to do with hit rates or exact entries. You will have success in trading if you understand that profits come in asymmetrically. If you are on the right track, your position should be big enough for you to benefit disproportionately. Your trading history might look like this:

-270

-1,745

+ 200

-2,340

+ 14,230

-3,140

+ 490

-1,300

-2,580

+ 45,360

-378

-1,700

And so on. I hope you understand the idea. The monster profits will only happen if you learn to buy consistently when you are on the right track.

Chapter 7
Go Global Macro

Since I recommend that traders should use of this method to observe the developments on the global markets, we should also look at the strategy that bears this name. The Global Macro Strategy is a hedge fund strategy, based on the macroeconomic principles of different countries or regions. For example, if the fund manager believes that the Eurozone is going into recession, he could sell short stocks or stock indices of the Eurozone. He has all the tools the financial sector has to offer at his disposal: stocks, futures, options, currencies, forwards, bonds or ETFs. Global macro funds thus build positions based on events or shifts in international financial markets worldwide.

One of the most famous Global Macro trades was the bet George Soros made against the British pound in 1992 (by the way, I do not share Soros political views, but I admire him as a trader). Soros then assumed that Great Britain would leave the European Monetary System. According to his analysis, in the UK, both inflation and the key interest rate were too high, which had a negative impact on the British economy. His fund then built up a short position of USD 10 billion in the British pound, over the course of several months. For the time, this was a huge position, even for a professional hedge fund. As you might know, Soros does not fiddle about on the edge – his strokes are broad. In the end, the UK had to give in, and leave the European Monetary System overnight. The pound depreciated dramatically. Soros' profit was over USD 1 billion, the biggest gain a trader had ever made on a single trade, till then.

Global Macro Traders have <u>a clear justification for their trades</u>. Now, such an approach sounds like you should have at least a degree in economics or a whole division of specialists who provide in-depth analyses of developments in the financial markets, from which you, the trader, can pick out the cream of the crop.

The truth is that the managers of these funds know just as little as you. Maybe they have access to more data than you do. Maybe they are a bit smarter (I'm not convinced about that!) But the fact is that these people are just as worried about whether the price of oil is likely to rise or not, or whether the UK will leave the EU or not, or whether President Trump will win the next election or not, and what this could mean to the dollar.

You actually have an advantage over these specialists. You are not accountable to any customers or investors, when it comes to your trading decisions. Customers can always threaten to withdraw their money if you do not perform well, and that can cost you your job. You do not have any of those problems. You can simply speculate fearlessly. The only thing you are risking is the money in your account.

And, with regard to the information that is available, we have much too much of it these days. The Internet is full of news, analyses and opinions from so-called specialists.

I specialize in crises. The reason for this is simple. At some point, you will hear about it, be it in the news or on one of your financial blogs on the Internet. Crises occur again and again, and sometimes they have long lead times that give you all the time in the world to find out and build up initial positions. When Greece skidded in 2010, the country was on the news every night (at least in Europe).

And you should not make it too complicated. If there's a crisis somewhere, your options are limited anyway. Do you want to go short in the currency of the country or do you prefer to short sell its most important stock index? Or both?

Whether or not you have detailed statistics and data on the country's problems is not going to make your decision-making process easier; on the contrary, it is more likely to paralyze you and maybe even prevent you from doing the trade at all. Surely, until now, nobody has become poor this way, but neither has it made anyone rich. Put simply: You will have to learn to be a speculator who acts internationally, despite limited information. Perhaps an awkward speculator in the beginning, but with increasing experience, you will become a more experienced speculator, and who knows? At some point, you might even become as shrewd as Soros, Rogers or Paulson.

Chapter 8

Look at the "Big Picture"

I'm always amazed at how little interest traders show in historical charts. If your main activity is the 5-minute chart, why look at a daily chart, let alone a weekly chart of your market?

But if you want to bet on bigger trends, then you should do just that: study long-term charts. You can find these charts on special websites, such as finviz.com. The nice thing about this site is the overview that it gives you, across all markets, at a glance. Just click on "futures" and then on "charts". You can see which markets are currently in an uptrend or a downtrend, and which ones are going sideways. Finviz lists the most important indices, commodities, bonds and currencies. It is enough if you visit this site once a week and are aware of what is going on in the markets right now.

Now, you may be wondering if it is absolutely necessary to study the price history of a market, not just for the last two or five years but, if available, also for the last 20 or 30 years, as some traders do.

I know a Dutch investor who goes back even further in time. He once invited me to his home, because he knew I was involved in the stock market. After chatting over a good cup of coffee, he invited me into an adjoining room, decorated with old maps, with a large oak table in the middle. He asked me to sit down, and then, he suddenly took several large, elongated notebooks out of a cupboard, and placed them on the oak table in front of me. As it turned out, he had compiled these books himself, with the utmost care. "There's only one copy of these in the world," he said. I was not quite sure whether he was joking, or if he had spoken with an ironic undertone. Anyway, I was amazed when I started leafing through one of the notebooks. Each sheet represented the historical price history of a market. He had the Dow Jones, the Dutch AEX, he had bonds, commodities and currencies. It was really fascinating, because some of his charts went back over 300 years in time.

This trader knew, for example, what the price of wheat was at the time of the French Revolution. He knew the price of coffee when the first coffee houses were opened in London and Paris in the seventeenth century. For gold and silver he needed two pages, because these charts went back over 800 years.

It was fascinating to see what this trader had put together, in the most laborious work. He had this information from a particular person who specializes in the presentation of such long-term charts.

You may be wondering how it is possible to have such chart histories, especially since the habit of grouping stocks together in an index did not materialize until the end of the 19th Century, when Charles Dow invented the Dow Jones Index. This was done by collecting the most important stock data before the index was introduced, thus calculating the Dow Jones backwards.

At first, I thought that his hobby, as he called it, was in fact a leisure activity, because what does it matter if you know today what the theoretical (recalculated) dollar price was at the time of the American War of Independence? The Dutch investor seemed to take it all very seriously (the Dutch, as we know, invented the stock market).

And the more I talked to him about this or that historical development in certain markets, the more I got the impression that he actually used his charts to speculate.

Of course, such calculations should be treated with some caution. As I flipped through his notebooks, he repeatedly pointed to one spot or another in an index or commodity chart and said, "I think it will take us another four or five years to reach that level. Then it will become interesting." I could see a little twinkle in his eyes at the thought. He left no doubt that he had the patience to wait four or five years before investing in this market or that.

Of course, you do not need to do your historical research as extensively as this Dutch investor did, but I was a bit jealous of his method. *He* has a perspective, I thought. I could imagine him sitting at his oak table every now and then, leaning over his charts and maybe thinking, "Okay, let us wait two more years before we do anything here."

I learned two things from this man. First, patience. Not only had he printed his charts (highly recommended), but he kept them like art books, so that he could look at them with the necessary respect and distance, in order to think about their development. This "Sunday perspective" gives him the necessary distance to look at something in peace. This is hardly possible on a screen.

The price phantasy that offers such a long-term perspective is even more important. If you look at a Dow Jones hourly chart (a perspective my Dutch stock market friend could only laugh at), how much price phantasy do you have? Five hundred points? A thousand?

This Dutch trader considered a Dow Jones of 25,000 points merely as an intermediate step on the way to 100,000 points. (When I was with him, the Dow stood at 9,000, I think). Because of his historical view, he had this price fantasy. He could not tell me exactly whether we would reach the 100,000 in 2040 or 2045, but he was pretty sure it would happen in about that period.

I am telling you this story, because it shows that without such price fantasies, you cannot become a successful speculator. You have to take a bird's-eye view and forget the daily back and forth on the stock market. All this is just noise, and it happens to confuse you.

To speculate, you need a clear mind and a perspective that deals more with weekly and monthly charts of a market than with hourly charts or even shorter time units. If you want to know where the money in the stock market is, that is where you will find it – in the weekly and monthly charts.

And if you're looking for clear entry or exit signals, I recommend using heikin ashi charts whenever possible, because they also filter the daily noise out of a chart. Here are some examples.

Image 4: USDCAD, weekly chart 2014 - 2016

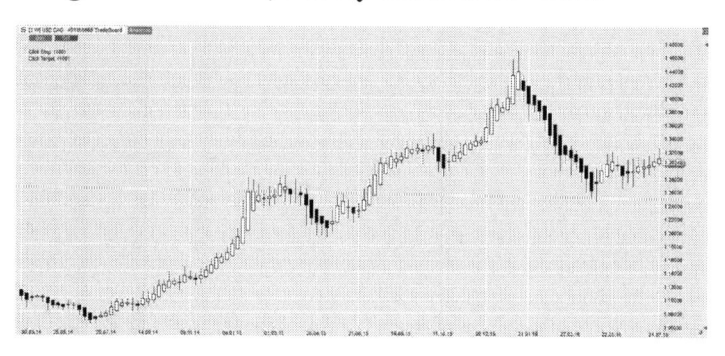

Look at this weekly chart of the US dollar/Canadian dollar currency pair. Each candle represents one week of trading. I think the trend on this chart is clear. As soon as the color changes, you can close the position or even trade in the opposite direction. If the color changes again, you should also close or change your position. Is it that easy? Yes, it is.

Image 5: Amazon, weekly chart 2015 – 2018

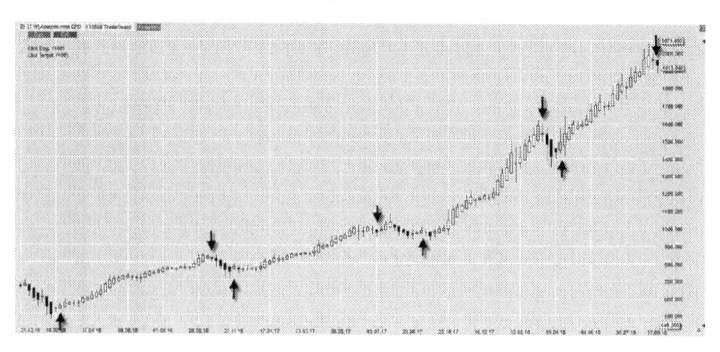

This weekly chart of the Amazon share may be even clearer. Sure, Amazon was in a clear upward trend during this period. But look how easily the heikin ashi candles could have helped you to build significant positions in such a market.

Image 6: Apple, weekly chart

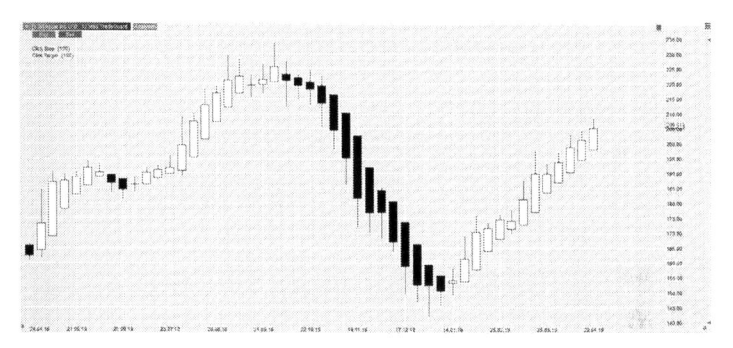

Or a current example. In the last quarter of 2018, Apple stock made a serious downward move (black Heikin Ashi Candles). But then, after a doji arose, the perfect entry signal for a long position came in January 2019.

Chapter 9

Look for a catalyst

Of course, you can go along with the trend, according to the examples in the previous chapter, but then you will actually be a trend follower. There is nothing wrong with that, but please do it with the market leaders, in other words, with the shares that are also being bought by the big funds. Then you have a good chance that your speculation will work out.

However, in the past, I often got really good results when I found a market that started moving because of a fundamental change. What else should move a market, if not some dramatic news, a positive or a negative?

In order for you to speculate on such a dimension, you need a catalyst. What do I mean by that? A catalyst is an event or development in a market, that fundamentally changes the perception of the players involved.

So, this is not a message that is going to push the price up or down a few percent in the short term. Not even a negative outlook or the downgrading of an analyst firm is enough to fundamentally change the perception of a company. Even "sudden" news (for example, a market approval of a drug in a biopharmaceutical company) will hardly help you. As a rule, the market opens up with a huge price gap after news like this. Thus, the news is already factored into the price. Of course, the stock might continue to rise, but there are no guarantees.

The same applies to surprisingly negative corporate news. Here, the stock opens with a discount down. Thus, the bad news is also factored in.

All these events are hard to predict and even harder to trade, unless you trade the technical countermovement. I described how to do that in my book "Trade Against the Trend". Short-term or unexpected news does not really help you when speculating on big trends. That's why you can confidently disregard them.

The same is true for surprising results of elections or referendums, as was the case with the Brexit. If, on the eve of such an event, you take a long or short position on the British pound, this is like gambling. You cannot really speculate on dramatic events such as the Francogeddon (red arrow on the left in the chart). That incident took just 25 minutes, and no one (or hardly anyone) expected it, especially as the Swiss National Bank had publicly announced, a few days earlier, that it would stick to the EUR/CHF peg of 1.20. Even central banks are run by human beings, and as you can see, they can change their minds anytime.

Image 7: EURCHF, weekly chart heikin ashi, 2014 - 2018

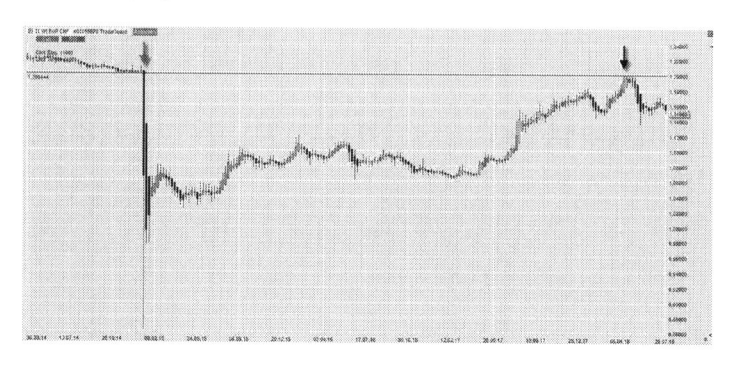

Of course, as an investor, you could have gradually built up a long EUR/CHF position, after the dust had settled in the Swiss franc debacle. It was safe to assume that the market had overreacted, and that it would correct the exaggeration (the EUR/CHF plunged from 1.20 to 0.96 within 25 minutes). This actually did happen, and the EUR/CHF actually reached exactly the lower edge of the former SNB peg (black arrow top right in the chart). However, the pair needed three years to do so. This violates our rule of wanting to grow our account fast. Such investments are interesting, but they usually take more time.

Anyone who knows me a bit, knows that despite all the information available on the Internet, I still like to read the newspaper. One may think that I am old-fashioned or a bit eccentric. Let me briefly explain the reason why I cling to this habit.

For the younger readers: a newspaper is an information medium printed on light paper, that is usually found hanging on a hook in good cafés.

When reading newspapers, the speculator should learn to filter out the messages that are important to him. Of course that's easier said than done. The old Hungarian speculator Andre Kostolany, whom I refer to here, taught that one should learn to read "between the lines". He meant that the actual news in itself is usually not interesting, because it is in the newspapers at the moment, so everyone knows about it.

When reading an article, a column (an opinion) or a commentary, you should pay attention to certain remarks or asides, because they may contain interesting information that you may have overlooked by merely skimming over the news. And that's why I actually recommend going to the coffee house every now and then, and grabbing an old-fashioned medium like a newspaper, because you still need to bring in <u>that necessary element of unhurriedness,</u> in order to even acknowledge such information. Unfortunately, you cannot smoke cigars in most cafés anymore (a weak-minded decision in my eyes), because that would slow down your reading pace even more. If I have the time to do this on my terrace at home on weekends, I often find that kind information – small comments or interesting asides that grab my attention as a speculator. It's exactly these remarks that can get a thought process going.

For example, the question might be: what effect could this event have on this market or that one?

As a current example (February 2019) the so-called *dieselgate* could apply. Several car manufacturers (especially Volkswagen) had carried out illegal manipulations, in order to circumvent the statutory limits for car exhaust emissions. That's the news.

Now, as a speculator, it is your job to think about what such an event might mean for the stock market. Of course, the immediate thought is to short sell the shares of the affected car manufacturers. The main candidate here was the German stock of Volkswagen, which was one of the main players in the scandal. However, if you look at the chart for this stock, you immediately realize that "the news" was factored in by the market within a very short time. The stock fell from EUR 168 to EUR 105 on the Frankfurt Stock Exchange, in just three days.

So here too the actual news doesn't help you much. The stock market reacts immediately and only smart day traders are able to benefit from such an event.

Volkswagen stock was therefore not of much value in terms of speculating on the diesel scandal. As Kostolany aptly said: "If you only read the headlines or the mostly boring annual reports, you will usually only learn what everyone already knows."

So, in connection with an event of such a dimension, you need to dig a little deeper if you want to find an idea that is interesting to speculate on. And indeed, in the months after dieselgate hit the news, there was an indirect profiteer. As this scandal gradually made it clear that diesel vehicles had fallen out of favor, there had to be other vehicle technology that would benefit. At first, of course, one thinks of electric vehicles, but that is still a very young market. Those who thought logically, came to the conclusion that initially, more gasoline cars would be purchased. The increased demand for gasoline cars eventually had consequences for the precious metal palladium, which is needed for the catalytic converters. Gasoline emissions are cleaned with palladium catalytic converters, and diesel emissions with platinum catalytic converters. Since the emissions regulations worldwide, but especially in China, had become more stringent, they required a higher proportion of palladium per catalytic converters. The results can be seen in the palladium chart. The arrow marks September 2015, when the dieselgate news broke. As you can see, it took some time for the market to change, but gradually, the insight prevailed among the market players, that a fundamental change had taken place. Investors also had plenty of time to position themselves in the market. You see, the new upward trend in palladium only became noticeable gradually. In this case, the catalyst for a stock market trend was literally the catalytic converter...

Image 8: Palladium 2015 -2019

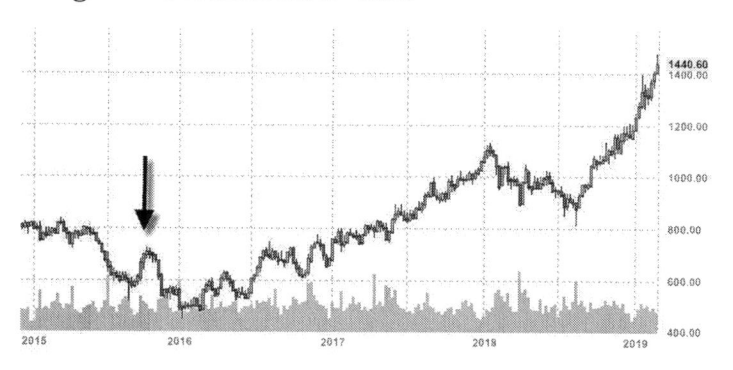

For comparison, the chart of Platinum in the same period:

Image 9: Platinum 2015 - 2019

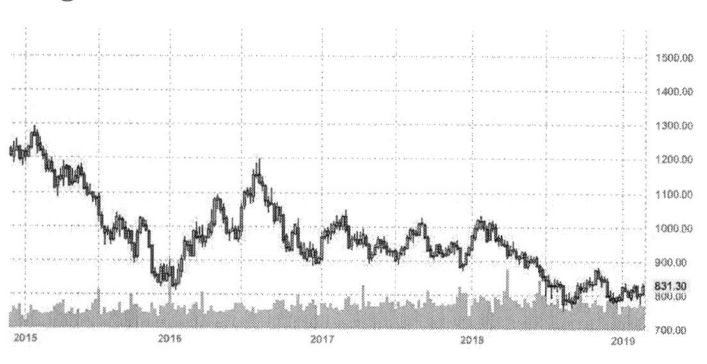

So you need a catalyst, an event that "moves" or fundamentally realigns a market for a while, as was the case with palladium.

Of course, the catalyst can also be politically motivated, for example, when presidential elections in the USA are imminent. American presidents or presidential candidates tend to be classed as stock-market friendly or stock-market-unfriendly. In the run-up to such elections, the stock market can rise, in the hope that the desired candidate (for investors) will win.

But even after the elections, the stock market can rise. This happened, for example, in November 2016 when, much to the surprise of many, Donald Trump moved into the White House. Since this was not expected by most analysts, they suddenly remembered Trump's attractive election promises for investors, such as generous tax cuts and all sorts of deregulation. The election results were followed by a veritable "Trump rally" in US stocks.

Wars can also become a catalyst. As the stock market anticipates future events, it often reacts or overreacts in the run-up to the expected event. This was the case in the weeks leading up to the second Iraq war in early 2003. The threats and the rattling of sabers in the media caused prices to tumble to the bottom. When the war began, as the first bombs fell on Baghdad, the stock market considered the matter to be over and done with, and it began to rise again.

This phenomenon can be observed again and again. Even in the run-up to the Second World War, it was no different. When the threat of war was imminent in 1939, the stock market fell. As soon as World War II began, stocks began to rise again. This phenomenon is described by the French term **"fait accompli"**. In English: accomplished fact. This moment occurs when all relevant news is factored into the price.

Why is that? Basically, <u>speculation can only be based on a future event</u>. So on something that *might* happen in the (near or distant) future. Therefore, a savvy speculator should direct his attention to the markets in which a future event is expected, hoped for or even feared. If all the news has been factored into the prices, and no further news is expected for the time being, what remains that could move the prices? And, of course, the more dramatic the event is or is likely to be, the more the prices will be exaggerated, until the market surrenders completely (down, as in the 2008 financial crisis) or skyrockets, as if there is no tomorrow (see Bitcoin 2017). There is no need to explain that the most money can be made in such markets.

The events do not always have to be so dramatic. If investors expect a company to deliver excellent quarterly results, they will buy the company's stock in advance. In general, this is a good opportunity for a speculation that lasts a few weeks. This method works particularly well with the current market leaders (i.e. the Apples, Alphabets, Facebooks and Amazons of this world, as of 2019). The speculator should close his position the day before the quarterly numbers come out. Quite often, investors will sell the stock on the day of publication, even if the results meet investors' expectations or for that very reason. Fait accompli!

Of course, the opposite also happens. If investors are pessimistic about the numbers, they sell the stock ahead of the release. If the numbers are better (or less dramatic) than expected, this news must be factored into the price. Often the stock then jumps and goes up for a few days. Such an event is rather less suitable for the method mentioned here. But it can be a good opportunity for short-term oriented traders.

The phenomenon can also be observed with regard to announcements by the central banks. If a central bank chief announces that he is going to raise rates, and this event is widely anticipated by market players, a multi-week rally will often start, even though interest rate hikes are generally negative for stocks. Here too:

fait accompli. If everyone knows that the central bank is going to raise interest rates, then this negative news (for equities) is already factored into the price. So stock prices can go up again. As you see, the stock market has its own logic, that you need to study if you want to be successful.

Why is the interest rate so important to the stock market? The increase in interest rates affects monetary growth. And the money factor is the oxygen that keeps the stock market alive. When the world's major central banks cut their key interest rates to almost 0% in the wake of the financial crisis, money became cheap and sought ways to be invested. Therefore, in the years following this measure, people were building houses like crazy with all this cheap money, and a lot of money was invested in stocks, because with the dividends, you could at least make a small profit.

Chapter 10
Mistakes to Learn From

After my silver trade, I wanted to repeat my coup. I will be honest. Since this success, I have made several mistakes , which I do not want to conceal from you. I speak of them here, so that the reader can learn from them, and hopefully not repeat them. I am not ashamed to have made these mistakes, though I am still a bit angry about them today. But, I hope that the trouble will be the fuel that ensures that I'm on the right side when the next opportunity comes around the corner.

Even though the events of that time (2008 financial crisis) occurred more than 10 years ago, it is still interesting to recall them. The mood at the time was so bad, that I assumed that every correction in gold and silver was an opportunity to buy. Not even close. After silver had reached a high in early March 2008, it fell continuously during the course of 2008. I bought silver again and again, and I had to close my positions at a loss each time. The result was, that at some point, I no longer dared to buy silver. And then the inevitable happened. Silver bottomed out at USD 9 at the end of 2008, and then it began to rise again in December. I was so annoyed by my losses that I did not dare to buy. A big mistake, as I found out later, because December 2008 was the starting signal of one of the largest bull markets in silver ever. Silver rose from USD 10 to almost USD 50 in just over two years, more than a fivefold increase! Although I traded silver in this period, I was never really able to benefit from this megatrend. And all that, even though I was able to take a good deal of the upward movement in 2007-2008. But, the subsequent movement in silver was ten times as big. You can figure out what I could have earned in such a market.

Image 10: Silver 2006 - 2019, Monthly Chart

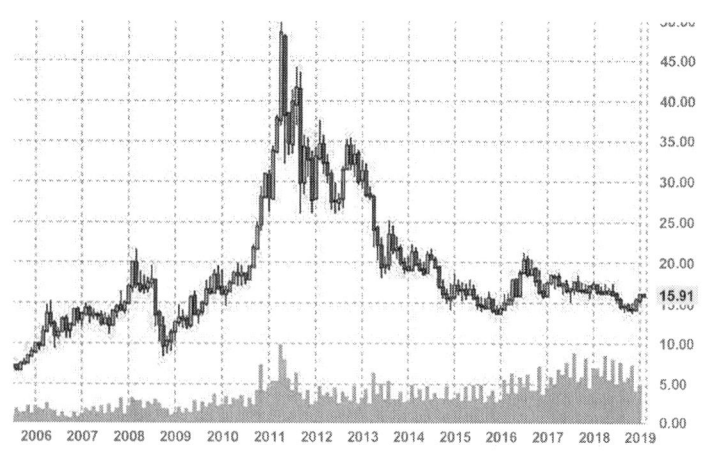

As if all that had not been enough, I tried to go to long in Silver after it had achieved its high in April

2011. You can clearly see in the chart how successful I was with this. To say I was a bit late with my silver trade would be a real understatement. I was so obsessed with silver that I did not see anything else. I thought the whole financial world was in a kind of permanent crisis after the so called financial crisis of 2008, so investing in gold and silver must be worth it. Not even close. The bull market in silver was over, and the only right thing to do would have been to take a short position. But I could not think that far at the time. I was fixated on "crisis" – so, silver and gold long! A big mistake!

The lesson I learned from this sounds simple. If you have had a big success in a market, it is best not to trade that market for a while, no matter what else happens. As a rule, you will take the wrong position the second time round, and lose money. The reason is simple. Emotionally, you are too dependent on this market. It has been good to you and has given you a decent profit. At the moment, in my experience, the most dangerous thing is to re-enter. It is better to look for an opportunity in another market.

Image 11: Dow Jones 2007 - 2019, monthly chart

As if this amateurish sting was not enough, I tried my luck in the stock markets in the months that followed. They had recovered well after the crash of 2008. In 2011, the Dow Jones had almost made up for the losses of the financial crisis. The stock markets had been rising for two years. Influenced by the Euro crisis (which was also the cause of the big rise in gold and silver), I was still in "crisis mode". I did not go long in the stock indices ... I went short. I thought this recovery would be a mistake. Meanwhile, the central banks had lowered interest rates to zero. So I should have known that investors could not make any money with government bonds. No capital going to fixed income usually means that it will seek other assets that at least bring some returns. And what could be more obvious than simply buying stocks and earning dividends. And so it happened. We have been in this bull market since March 2009. (As of May 2019). The charts also show it unmistakably, especially the charts of the American stock indices. But instead of going long and just buying the trend and making serious money, I went short! What a mistake!

I am telling you this, because these stupidities are not that unusual. <u>Sometimes it is really hard to just do the obvious thing.</u> From 2009 to 2019, we had one of the biggest bull markets in stocks in history. So we had 10 years to go long and make money. Over the years, countless crash prophets have called for the end of this bull market. "It's not possible!". "It's all bought on credit!". "This is a central bank rally that has no substance!". You can expand the list of reasons, as to why you should not buy any shares during this time, indefinitely.

There was a good reason why Jesse Livermore tried, by all means available, to block his ears, especially to analysts – all those tips, and the people who think they know it all. Nobody knows anything. This has to be clear. Like Livermore, I recommend that you listen to nobody and that you certainly do not waste your time with endless analyses and opinions. That is hard. I did not follow my own advice, and that cost me a lot of money. Believe what you see, and not the opinions of others. It is better to watch the development of the long-term charts. If a stock index has been rising for two years, and it continues to rise, is there any reason to go short?

Chapter 11
Success with cotton

I was unable to benefit from the bull market in silver in 2011, but I succeeded with another speculation, which corresponded better to my skeptical nature. Hence the following story.

A friend of mine, who lived in Berlin at that time, had a small textile company, with its production site in a small town in the federal state of Brandenburg, in the east of Germany. This fact alone amazed me, because, in 2010, there were not many textile companies that were able to produce in any of the former East German states, with their high unemployment figures. Rather, one would have expected the production sites to be in countries like Bangladesh. My friend's company made industrial textiles, mostly workwear for hospitals. It was a niche in which she had managed to assert herself over the years, with the help of a loyal team. I really admired her for this achievement. Engaging people in that weak economic environment by making clothes. Hats off!

We met for a cup of coffee, and I remember that we also talked about her company from time to time. At the end of 2010, she called me, asking if I had time to talk. She knew that I was involved in the stock market. She sounded restless on the phone. When I met her a day later, she looked very worried. At first I thought that her company had run out of clients, and that she would have to dismiss employees. That had happened in the past. It turned out, however, that her concern was quite different. "I have several sales orders", she said, "but I cannot deliver." "Why?" I asked. "Normally, you always deliver punctually." "Yes," she said. "That's not the problem. I cannot get any cotton. We're desperately waiting for a delivery, but it's just not coming, so we cannot produce." "No cotton?" I said. "How can that be? Cotton is as plentiful as sand on the beach."

I thought it was.

She put on her worried face again, and then she began to inform me about what was going on in the cotton market. Apparently, there was a big shortage of cotton. Apparently! When she started to explain the situation to me, I got a little lesson in the world of raw materials. All around the world, cotton is harvested during different seasons. Then it is processed and transported to the spinning mills. In that year there was a weak harvest in the important production country, Pakistan. Demand had grown steadily in the previous years. Especially China, with its hot economy, was hungry for all kind of commodities, including cotton.

In addition, there were export restrictions, and as if that was not enough, producers in Pakistan and India began to hoard their supplies, due to steadily rising prices. "They simply are not handing over the cotton anymore," my friend said in a desperate tone. "They would rather fill their warehouses, in the hope that prices will rise even further. The situation is desperate."

In fact, the price of cotton on the Intercontinental Exchange in New York had risen by more than 160% in one year. At the time when my friend made me aware of the problem, the price of a pound of cotton stood at USD 1.68. When I looked at the chart at home, her problem became clear to me. In the preceding years, the price had fluctuated between USD 0.40 and USD 0.80 per pound. There was no problem getting cotton at that time. Actually, there was always enough cotton, but the exceptional demand from China and the weak harvest had fueled the price. It was an extraordinary situation. When the producers began to hoard, there seemed to be no cotton available. This was, of course, an artificially induced shortage, but it brought small textile companies, like that of my friend, to the brink of insolvency.

For a speculator, such information is worth its weight in gold. I could read the seriousness of the situation (and the utter exaggeration in the price) in my friend's eyes. Her desperation actually told me everything. She had orders in her books. Heck, the customer was waiting for his workwear, but she could not produce, let alone deliver, because she could not get cotton anymore, although the warehouses of the producers in India and Pakistan were overfull. This information was served to me on a tray.

Image 12: Cotton, 2005 - 2019, Monthly chart

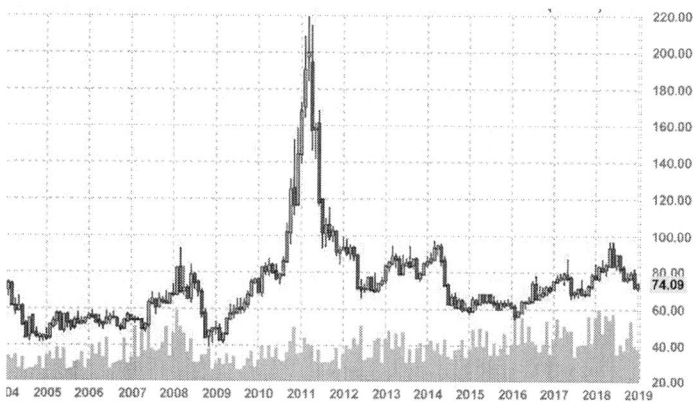

I had never dealt with the cotton market before. As I began to study the cotton futures chart in the final weeks of 2010, I realized that I had come to the party too late. The chart had already built a parabolic slope. To enter the last phase of a bull market did not seem advisable to me. Since I was pretty much bearish at the time anyway, I decided to keep watching the futures on cotton and eventually go short.

In January 2011, the price of cotton finally rose above USD 2.00, attaining a high of USD 2.25 in February. I watched the future every day to see signs of weakness.

When I realized that a price above USD 2.00 was not sustainable, I went short with a first position, just under USD 2.00. The position immediately went into profit and was never in danger. Encouraged by this confirmation, I opened further short positions, which also went into the plus relatively fast. The volatility was extreme and the PL (profit - loss) on my platform changed to my favor or disfavor, faster than you could imagine. Not for the faint hearted!

Unsurprisingly, due to the twisted "mood", the first bearish news for cotton came in. Instead of the expected demand of 120 million tons for 2011, expectations were revised downwards. Only 113 million tons were expected. Demand began to slow down, first and foremost from China. As if that was not enough, the first reports of very good harvests came in. India expected an increase in production of 255,000 tons. Similar news came from West Africa, Turkey and Greece. Of course, that was news that did not really give the cotton price wings, so to speak. On the contrary. Although there was a technical correction in April, I remained short and even expanded my position. My assumption that the upward movement of 2010 would be completely corrected, was confirmed. In June, the price finally reached the USD 1.00 level. The price had thus more than halved. I gradually began buying back contracts to close my position. Once again, it was an incredible ride, but I managed to make a decent profit with the cotton crash. I had never been able to trade such a downtrend and come away feeling quite satisfied, though my enthusiasm was somewhat subdued by my previous bad investments in the stock market.

I called my friend and asked her how things were going. Everything was fine, she said, cotton was readily available again and her company was able to produce and deliver on time.

Although my short cotton position is unlikely to have had much influence on the price, I modestly helped to push the price down. This corrected the bubble, which was ultimately the result of an artificial shortage. This time, the real evil speculators were certainly not the short sellers, but clearly the greedy producers, who hoarded more and more cotton, due to the rising prices, thereby fueling the price even further. The cotton crisis of 2010-2011 was really life-threatening for my friend's company. Of course, you cannot consider her report as insider information about a particular market. She was far too helpless herself at that moment. But the story taught me that such "crises" may well contain valuable information, especially emotionally vivid information that may offer the opportunity for successful speculation. It pays to go through the world with your eyes and ears open.

Chapter 12
My ruble trade

It is well known to every trader, that the price of oil is an important factor on the world stage. It is therefore essential that you keep an eye on it, as well as on other important indicators, such as the dollar or the yield curve of US government bonds. Whenever capital is withdrawn somewhere, and flows to another place, it is often because something important is happening in one of those indicators.

Image 13: Oil price, monthly chart 2003 - 2019

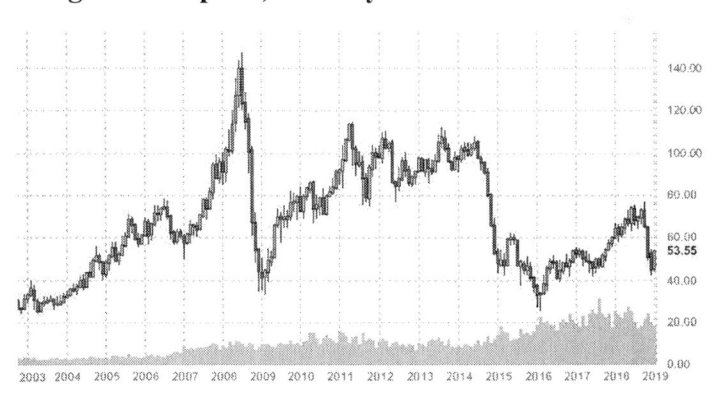

Between 2007 and 2008, the oil price was in a spectacular bull market (an excellent chance to make a fortune, by the way). After rising to over USD 140 a barrel, the price plunged below USD 40 a barrel, after the financial crisis. It was an unprecedented crash that took just six months (again an excellent opportunity to make a fortune with short positions). Between 2009 and 2014, the oil price recovered and reached a price of USD 100 again. Then all became quiet. Oil seemed to stabilize at that level. Technically speaking, it formed an extended symmetrical triangle. If you ask me, this is not a very reliable technical pattern. There were smaller breakout attempts to the upside, all of which failed. I was already lurking in the shadows, because I assumed that oil would eventually break out to attack the highs of 2008. However, this did not happen, and the price continued to go sideways at around the USD 100 level in the first two quarters of 2014.

And as so often happens on the stock exchange, when the expectation of market actors (including myself) is not fulfilled: the opposite happens. Oil broke out of this sideways pattern on the downside in the summer of 2014. The crash was not as spectacular as in 2008. But still, a slide from USD 100 to USD 27 is spectacular. That's a loss of value of 73%!

I have to admit that I was completely surprised by this crash. Once again, I had been deceived by my expectations. The price of oil just had to rise, because "the world" needed more oil and the supply was becoming scarcer (I thought). I could just watch the oil price going down day by day. That is what you have to deal with when you have certain expectations, and then the opposite happens. You can only stand on the sideline and watch. But it got even worse. I did not get in (not even with a small test position), because I assumed it was a false breakout. I expected the market players to suddenly take a 180 degree turn. In the end, this did not happen. It was a real breakout, and the price of oil continued to fall.

Of course, the analysts were soon on the spot with their explanations. There was more oil than everybody thought! How interesting! As if this oil had not existed in 2012 and 2013, when oil was stable, at above USD 100 a barrel. The second explanation also seemed obvious. This time the Americans, more specifically the shale oil boom, had caused the price collapse. In just a few years, the US had become the largest oil producer in the world, relieving itself of its dependence on Saudi Arabia. All this seemed to catch the market players' attention in July 2014, although they couldn't have cared less about what the Americans were doing in May and June. You see, the analysts always have their explanatory models ready. But they do not take them out of the drawer until the market begins to confirm their assumptions.

That autumn of 2014, I pondered as to how I could still benefit from this movement. The opportunity came, but from a very different side than I expected. I should have known, but it did not dawn on me until the first news broke, that the Russian ruble was in trouble.

What does the ruble have to do with oil? Pretty much. Two-thirds of Russia's exports are oil and natural gas, and the gas price is mostly geared to the price of oil. Half of the Russian taxes come from these sources.

There are also some other countries that are heavily dependent on oil prices, Canada, for example. And indeed, the Canadian dollar also slipped in the fall of 2014, against most other currencies, most notably the dollar. A long position in the USD/CAD seemed the logical consequence (Long US Dollar, Short Canadian Dollar).

But for some reason, I was more interested in the Russian ruble. It was a currency I had not traded before. It does not belong to what you can call the usual trading instruments, basically because the spread on the spot markets is far too high. The ruble had indeed depreciated against the dollar in September and October.

Image 14: USD/RUB, daily chart, September-December 2014

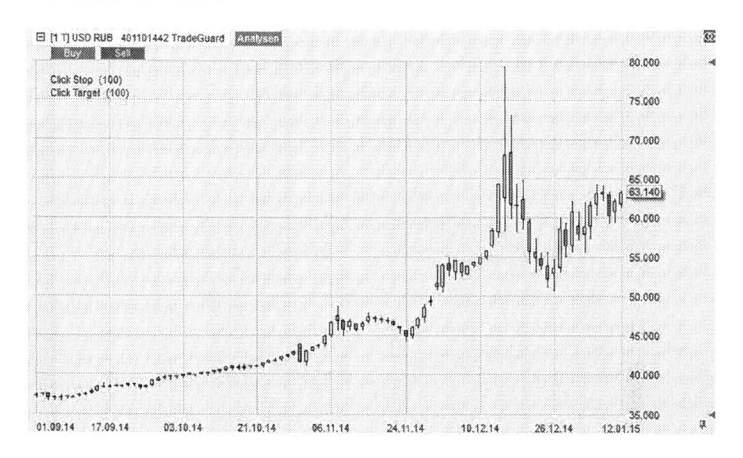

The USD/RUB pair rose from 35.00 to 42.00-43.00 in September-October 2014 (in the case of the USD – Russian ruble exchange rate, rising prices meant that the US dollar was appreciating and the ruble was depreciating). There had been an upward trend. But there was still no sign of an emerging buying frenzy (selling frenzy for the ruble). However, this changed in early November, as volatility increased significantly and the USD/RUB suddenly rose to 48.00. I bought a first test position at the end of October, at 43.00, and felt that my assumption that the ruble could continue to depreciate had been confirmed.

Of course, there were reasons for the crash of the ruble. The West imposed economic sanctions on Russia, in the wake of the Ukraine crisis (Crimea), which were now beginning to take effect. Well, the

2014 ruble crisis was not the first. During the last ruble crisis in 1998, it was already all about oil, and this time, the further crash of the oil price in the last quarter of 2014 seemed to accelerate the fall of the ruble. The Russian oligarchs withdrew their money from their Russian accounts and placed it in dollars, Swiss francs or euros. When the smart money gets out, it accelerates the depreciation of the currency.

During the course of November, I started to expand my position, although the ruble mostly went sideways. I even had some losses, as the USD/RUB fell back to 45.00 in late November. I was thinking about reducing my position when the USD/RUB started to rise towards the 50.00 mark in the last few days of November. I started buying again. Meanwhile, the price of oil had fallen below USD 70 and was heading towards the USD 60 mark. For the first two weeks of December, the USD/RUB continued to rise, reaching 55.00, which prompted me to further expand my short position in the ruble. I now had serious profits.

Finally, on the December12, the 55.00 level was conquered and the USD/RUB appeared to be heading towards 60.00 in the third week of December. 60 rubles to a dollar! In Russia, queues formed in front of the exchange offices, because everyone wanted to get rid of their rubles. People began to spend their money and bought electronic devices, cars and nonperishable foods. A scenario set in, similar to the situation in 1998, when the Russians lost confidence in their own currency.

Of course, the Russian central bank stepped in – the central banks are always the most important players in the matter. On December 11, they raised the key interest rate from 9.50 to 10.50%. The central bankers stepped in, although as recently as October, they had raised the key interest rate by 150 points, due to an expected rise in inflation rates. Contrary to their expectations, this measure could not stop the fall of the ruble. The market had obviously expected a larger move in the interest rate. The ruble fell further. Although there were rumors that the central bank had intervened in the foreign exchange market several times, but that did not stop the downward move of the ruble.

After the weekend, the decline of the ruble continued. The USD/RUB rose to 64.00. The rate hike of the previous Thursday had no effect. I kept buying and waiting. On Monday night, President Putin finally intervened, forcing the central bank to raise the key rate from 10.5 to 17.00 percent. That was a huge increase in the interest rate. It was the same measure that had been taken in 1998, to stem the ruble crisis of the time. On the Tuesday after Putin's intervention, the volatility was insane. The USD/RUB was swinging between 60 and 78. Within minutes, I was thousands richer or poorer.

It was clear that the market had been waiting for Putin to intervene. Only, nobody knew how the ruble would react. I watched with fascination, as the USD/RUB rose to 78.00. Therefore, I had huge gains with my position. However, during the day, the pair fell sharply and it dawned on me that we might be experiencing the final act of the drama. I've learned by now, that if the chart goes parabolic and the volatility gets insane, it's usually a sign that we may have seen the highs.

I started selling, admittedly not at the best prices. Everyone, of course, wants to sell at the high, although it must be clear that this is impossible. No one knows where the high of this move will be, ultimately. I began to systematically scale out my position. After all, I had made considerable profits. I sensed that Putin's radical intervention might be a turning point. The ruble had already devalued vastly, and the possibility of economic sanctions from the West, and the crash of the oil price, were factored in.

I kept part of the position, in case even this drastic measure did not work. This assessment proved to be wrong. Although the USD/RUB rose above 70.00 again on Wednesday, it was unable to hold the level on Thursday and Friday, so I closed the position completely.

At this point, let me say that some readers may regard this kind of speculation as morally reprehensible.

You can see it either way. You can either consider a speculation against the ruble as a reprehensible act, to the detriment of the Russian people, or you can consider the devaluation of the ruble as a necessary correction of the market, in order to force the Russian leadership to take measures to regain control of the rampant inflation. After all, such a dependency on crude oil is not a healthy basis for a stable economy in Russia in the longer term. The market is forcing Russia to reconsider this position. For one thing is clear, as long as this dependency exists, any fall in the price of oil will put the ruble under pressure. The devaluation of the ruble was necessary for the Russian economy, just as the decline in the cotton price ultimately had a positive effect on the textile industry (it was to the detriment of greedy producers who would have been happy to see even higher cotton prices).

You can argue any way you like. As a speculator, it is not your job to save the Russian economy. There are always two sides to trading and speculating: buyers and sellers, and as long as you consider it morally reprehensible, that there must be a seller in every transaction, you have not understood why the stock market is even necessary. Sometimes you stand on this side, and sometimes on the other side. If you want to make money, your job is to be on the right side more than you are on the wrong side. That's all!

Chapter 13
Thanks to Presidents Erdogan and Trump!

In 2017, I already had an eye on the Turkish Lira. The inflation rate in Turkey had risen to 13%. That's high, but not unusual for an "emerging economy", as Turkey is. The lira began to depreciate in 2017, but all of this took place within a reasonable range.

Image 15: EUR/TRY, February - September 2018

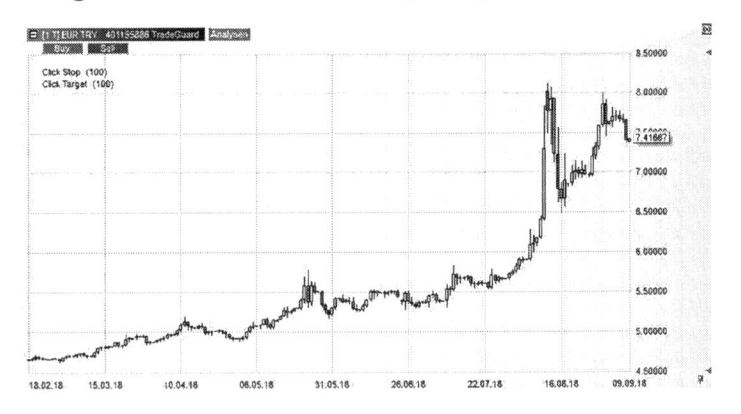

From March 2018, the lira began to depreciate a bit more And in April 2018, when it jumped over the 5 lira per euro mark, I went long with a first position in the EUR/TRY currency pair (With the Euro-Turkish lira currency pair, rising prices mean that the Euro appreciates and the Turkish lira devalues). I had to be patient. The lira hovered around the 5,000 mark for the remainder of the month and even dipped below that mark towards the end of the month, putting my position a little bit in the red. Since the loss remained manageable, I kept the position.

In May, the devaluation of the lira accelerated. As soon as the level of 5 lira per euro had been reconquered, I bought a second position. I was rewarded for my courage, because soon the pair climbed in the direction of 5.5000, which gave me several thousand Euros in profits.

The causes for the devaluation were varied as always. Probably the most important thing to me were the rising interest rates in the USA. In the months before, this had led to significant outflows of capital from the so-called "emerging markets" to the United States. This was especially the case for countries like South Africa, Argentina, Brazil and Turkey. As the Fed began raising interest rates, I realized that this would lead to a general devaluation of the currencies that had hitherto lived off the US low interest rate policy. Above all, the Turkish economy profited from these capital inflows. The current account deficit of Turkey was (and is) especially large. In short, that means that the upswing of the Turkish economy in the years before was largely built on credit.

Another accelerator was the refusal of the Turkish central bank to raise interest rates, which is the usual monetary policy instrument to fight inflation and the devaluation of its own currency. This refusal was not voluntary, but rather due to pressure from President Erdogan. Normally, the central bank should act independently of the policy (it is not to be assumed that any politician who happens to become president also understands monetary policy). In the case of Turkey, the central bank was considered independent, that fell away, de facto, after Erdogan's election victory. Erdogan publicly stated that interest rates that were not determined by him were the "father and mother of all evil." As the reader might know, interest-based banking is banned in Islam.

As the devaluation of the lira accelerated further in May 2018, the central bank was only able to prevent a further decline by raising its base rate by 300 basis points, from 13.5% to 16.5%. Although this led to a temporary recovery of the lira, the currency continued to trade above 5 lira per euro level. On the days after the jump in the interest rate, my position suffered, but it was never really in danger. Of course, I expected an intervention by the Turkish central bank, despite Erdogan's rhetoric. A clear increase in interest rates was a signal to the markets (and to me). However, the lira did not recover significantly. It did not even recover when Erdogan announced that he wanted to bring the presidential and parliamentary elections forward to June 2018.

On June 7, the Turkish Central Bank announced that it would raise rates again, by 125 basis points. Although this led to some gains for the lira, it did not impress the market in any way. On June 14, Erdogan tightened his rhetoric against "the financial markets" by threatening to act against the rating agency Moody's after the elections. This, of course, was a ridiculous statement of no importance, to which the lira responded with another devaluation of a good 1,000 pips.

When Erdogan's AKP finally won the elections, and Erdogan had a clear majority in parliament, the lira did not recover either. On the contrary. When he boldly announced that interest rates would soon be falling in Turkey, the devaluation of the lira began to accelerate all the more.

Although EUR/TRY continued to move sideways in June and early July, it was stable above 5,500 from mid-July, which encouraged me to buy more positions. Somehow I knew I was on the right path. It was becoming clearer and clearer that it was Erdogan himself who was going to talk his own currency into the ground. I could not have chosen a better ally than the Turkish president for my speculation against the lira.

And it continued! On July 9, he appointed his own son-in-law as minister of the new finance ministry. Erdogan empowered himself, through a presidential decree, to appoint the Governor of the Central Bank. By doing so, he definitively abrogated the independence of the central bank, although it was already de facto. I became more and more aware that some people in Ankara were really starting to panic. The more Erdogan seized the course of the monetary policy, the sooner he undermined the meagre remaining stability of his currency.

On July24, the Turkish central bank announced that, despite a renewed rise in inflation, it would leave interest rates at 17.75%. This led to a renewed sell-off in the lira, as well as on the Turkish stock market.

Everything went according to plan for me, although a real catalyst was still missing, in order to catapult the EUR/TRY really up. I sensed that it would come, I just did not know from which corner. And I could not have guessed that it would be President Trump, who would really get my speculation against the lira going.

More specifically, it was not Trump himself, but an American pastor of the Evangelical Presbyterian Church, named Andrew Brunson, who would eventually bring me a sizeable profit! Brunson moved to Turkey in 1993 and founded a small Church of the Resurrection in Izmir. When he wanted to renew his visa in 2016, he was arrested. He was accused of espionage and support for the banned PKK in Turkey. In 2017, the US demanded the release of the pastor. Erdogan's offer was an exchange. He would release Brunson if the US surrendered Fethullah Gülen to Turkey. Gülen lived in exile in the US, and was believed, by the Turkish, to be responsible for the coup attempt of July 15, 2016.

The tug of war between the two countries, surrounding the American pastor, created a tense relationship between the two countries, which eventually led to a veritable diplomatic conflict. On August 9, Erdogan delivered a speech proclaiming, "If they have their dollars, we have our people, our righteousness and our God." Hereby he squandered any hope of economic reform and a monetary policy that did justice to the facts. The reaction of the market was clear. The lira depreciated again and the EUR/TRY rose to 6.15.

Looking at the chart, which had gone parabolic in the last few hours and catapulted the gains of my position into the six-figure range, I sensed that the end was near. No one knows in advance where the high will be, just as nobody can predict the low. When the EUR/TRY finally shot up like a rocket on August 10, rising to an incredible 7.83, I started scaling out my position in the late hours of August 10, unaware that we were actually seeing the highs in EUR/TRY for that moment. Of course, I did not manage to sell at the high again. I was able to get rid of some contracts at a fantastic price of 7.50, others at a slightly lower price. It was a fabulous profit. Although EUR/TRY rose over 8.00 the next day, I could only watch it doing so. I was completely out. When EUR/TRY fell back below 6.50 in the days after, I was quite satisfied. Perhaps I should have sent thank-you cards to the Presidents Erdogan and Trump. Because it was their play-acting that enabled this huge gain for me.

Chapter 14
Speculating with stocks

An important question that arises now is whether this method works just as well with stocks. The answer is clear: yes. There are plenty of examples of traders who have become rich by buying a particular stock and systematically expanding their position as the price of the stock developed in their favor.

You do not need to get in at the start of the movement. Of course, each of us would like to have bought Apple in 1998 and then held on until 2019. The likelihood that you will succeed doing it like this is infinitely small. Besides, the question here is not how to become wealthy slowly, but how to grow a small account fast. You can do this if you trade Apple, Amazon or Facebook for a few months.

I would even say that this is an excellent method. So, do not look for some obscure Kazakhstan stock to do it with. Stick to the current market leaders, because then you will be trading with the big funds that do exactly the same thing as you. The likelihood of a trend turning here is much smaller, unless the market players' perception of a company were to change abruptly, which usually does not happen quickly with companies that have a good business model.

Image 16: Amazon, weekly chart August 2017 - September 2018

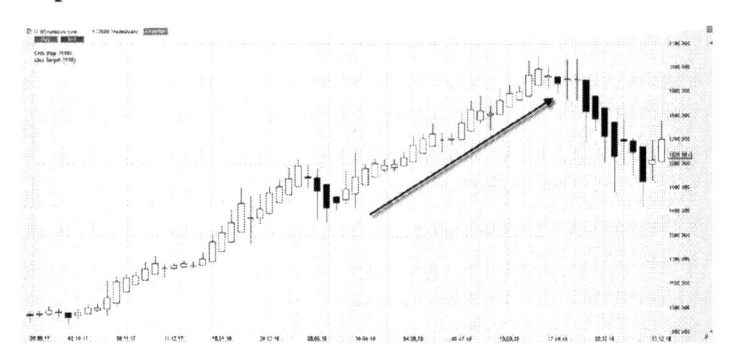

If, for example, at the end of April 2018, after the minor correction, you entered Amazon at a price of USD 1,500 and held out until September, when Amazon finally reached USD 2,000 (arrow on the chart), that USD 500 price gain would have been enough to make a fortune. In addition, you had four months to gradually expand your position and trade with the market's money.

To better visualize the big market leaders' trends, I like to use the heikin ashi chart, especially the weekly chart. As you can see from the example of the Amazon stock, there was hardly any technical correction during this movement from USD 1500 to USD 2000.

This is typical of stocks that have a large following. Therefore, you should trade exactly these stocks if you want to implement the strategy that I propose in this book. This is where the best chances for success are. On the chart, you can see how the big funds trade the stock. Every minimum loss day is an invitation to buy the stock. On a weekly basis, you hardly notice it. The heikin ashi charts help you stay in the stock, even if it goes in the other direction for a few days.

Image 17: Apple, Weekly Chart, July 2016 November 2017

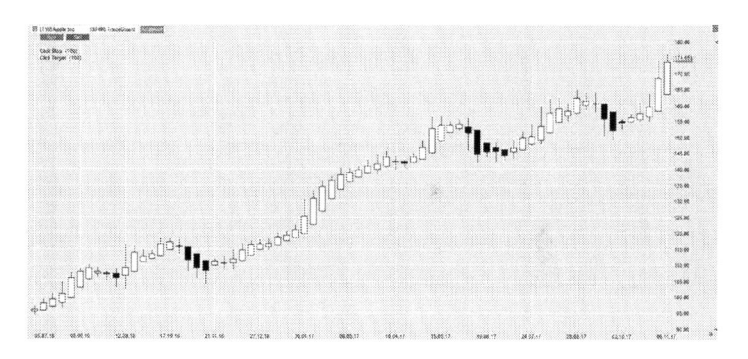

This weekly chart from Apple shows clearly why you should trade the market leaders. The liquidity in these stocks is so big that the chance for random reversals or corrections is very small. If the market players involved in such a phase come up with the idea of selling the stock suddenly, it will be due to clearly bad news from the company or a negative outlook for the next few quarters. That's why it makes sense to trade such a stock from the reporting season to the next reporting season. In between there are sometimes excellent trend phases that can take several months. As a speculator you can benefit from these trend phases. So you do not have to buy the stock and hang onto it for years.

If you prefer stocks rather than general markets, then you should trade stocks. Of course, you should be aware that stocks are the securities of a company, and companies are run by people who can withhold information from market players. I do not claim that such a scenario cannot happen in the general markets too. The difference is, if you trade an index like the Dax, the CAC40, the Dow Jones, or the Bovespa, you have no management risk as you have when trading a single stock. You always have a market risk, and I do not deny that an event such as the Flash Crash of 2012 could not happen again. That is why I say that you have to write off the money for each specific speculation in advance.

However, it seems to me that the risks involved in trading general markets such as stock indices, commodities or currencies, are lower than when trading in individual stocks.

There is another reason why I prefer to trade markets rather than stocks, even though they may have strong trends. If you trade the Alphabets, Apples and Amazons of this world, because they are going up, you are basically doing trend following. You follow the trend in the hope that it will continue for a while. Now, trend following is a legitimate way to earn money on the stock market. But it is usually a slow method. There is nothing wrong with that either, but as we want to grow our small account fast, we are violating the "fast" rule with trend following.

You will have noticed this from the examples of trades that I have carried out. For speculation, I usually choose a market in which <u>some kind of crisis is going on.</u> I favor situations in which something comes to a head. The reason is simple. Such markets <u>are prone to exaggerations</u>, and if I'm well-positioned, I usually benefit disproportionately from such situations.

That was the case with silver (financial crisis 2008). That was the case with the ruble crisis and the lira crisis. In all such crises, what happens is that the market overreacts. It's usually noticeable that the chart starts to rocket or build a parabolic rise (or starts to fall in the case of a downtrend).

And when a chart assumes parabolic shapes, I know that the end is near. Then the time has come to realize the profits. However, the specific main factor of my method is that the vast majority of profits are realized in the last, and often dramatic, days of the "crisis". Why? Because in the weeks and months leading up to it, I have built up my position step by step and I am fully invested in the moment when "the exaggeration" really starts and the market "overreacts". At that moment, I want to have my biggest position.

Of course, if you simply follow the trend, you can also make good profits, but often not as much as you could achieve in the kind of crises I am talking about here. That's why I favor crisis markets, because they promise me the biggest possible profit.

That leads me to perhaps the most important reason why I prefer this method when it comes to growing my account fast. This method is designed for people who have a winning mentality and who know how to make the most of the extraordinary opportunities that the stock market offers now and then. This is an attitude that is more about maximizing profits than avoiding loss and risk. If you go to the stock exchange with the mindset of not wanting to lose, you will lose. But if you go with the absolute will to win, then you have good chances of winning. Is it really that simple? Yes, it is.

Chapter 15
Trade what you see

As a speculator, you should try to be honest – at least to yourself. If I report some success here, it does not mean that I should not admit my mistakes as well. I have been wrong more often than I have been right. For example, I mentioned that I tried to short the Dax and Dow Jones several times between 2010 and 2012, even though we were clearly in a bull market. Actually I knew it too well. Looking at the long-term chart, it showed me that the long sideways phase of the years 2000-2009 in the Dow Jones was over.

And I had a good argument too. If the Fed lowers interest rates to zero, you can barely make any money with bonds. What does the manager of a large fund do in this case? Exactly! He increases his equity quota, because in equities, he can at least earn a return on the dividends. I knew it, and I even publicly proclaimed it at a podium discussion for investors in Brussels. Each speaker was asked to make a forecast for a market. I showed the audience a long-term chart of the Dow Jones on a big screen.

And I showed them an upward price projection. Based on my analysis at this conference in 2010, I prophesied a Dow Jones of 20,000 points (the Dow Jones stood at about 10,000 points in 2010). One half of the audience looked at me skeptically, the other half just laughed. I saw my "colleagues" at the table on the podium shake their heads.

The point was, I did not say this in the US, but in Europe. In the US, traders had already been back on the bull train for a while, while the Europeans were in the midst of the so-called "euro crisis". The media in Europe was full of negative news and you could feel it in the general mood in the audience at that conference. People were so paralyzed by the negativity that they could not see the obvious opportunities in the US. I was laughed at, and nobody wanted to talk to me after the panel discussion. Who wastes time on a charlatan and fantasist?

Honestly, that did not hurt me much. Much worse was that I did not follow my own convictions with deeds. Instead of just going long in the American stock market and building long-term positions in the biggest bull market in history and making a fortune, I went short. Multiple times...

How can you explain this kind of behavior? How can one act against his own conviction?

I have no real answer to this even today. <u>I know that the obvious is often the hardest thing to do.</u> We humans are apparently conditioned to prefer the more complicated path, because it seems more logical or plausible to us. Simply buying stocks when they go up, in order to sell them a few years later at high profits, just seems too simplistic for us. But believe me, most of the wealth in the stock market was made exactly that way – by having people do the obvious. Just as it was obvious to me to short the lira when Erdogan broke his own currency, and just as it was obvious to short the Russian ruble when oil prices dropped dramatically.

The obvious, however, does not have a lot of fans, as I learned at the investors conference in Brussels. Well, obviously I could not convince them – I did not even believe in my own prophecy, otherwise I would not have gone short, contrary to my own conviction.

At that moment one should remind the words of Jesse Livermore, who did his utmost to ignore the opinions and tips of his colleagues, so that they could not tarnish his judgment. If it was hard to accomplish this at the beginning of the century, it is almost a heroic act to keep yourself away from all of that in our completely networked times.

Most people seek confirmation for their actions. Is that what I'm doing right now? Maybe there are others who see it exactly the same way as I do. Maybe we can do this together? In a group? I hope the reader can see the absurdity of this idea.

Yes, it is uncomfortable to do the opposite of what a whole bunch of investors in a conference hall – who even laugh at you. But that's exactly what you should do. And do not make it unnecessarily difficult. If you have an idea or see an opportunity somewhere, then just buy a small test position. This will show you whether you are in the right market or not. And do not forget the words of the Hungarian speculator Andre Kostolany. <u>It's not the news that makes the price, but the price that makes the news.</u> If there is a crisis somewhere, then you can assume that at some point, the negative news will appear, trying to "explain" it all away. The same is true of the positive news, when something begins to rise dramatically.

Chapter 16
How and When Should You Buy?

Some traders will wonder how to go about progressively building a position in a market that is rising or falling dramatically. There is no right or wrong here. If you are right with your assessment, <u>then your position cannot be big enough</u>.

We tend to underestimate the factor of position size when speculating, although it is the more important than anything else. In my opinion, whether your hit rate is 30%, 50% or even 70%, only plays a minor role. The question of <u>how big your position is, if you are right,</u> is much more important. As I said before, I do not think it's a drama to lose on your first two attempts, for example, if you lose USD 2,000 twice, and make USD 40,000 on your third attempt. In that case, your hit rate is a meager 33.33%. But your average profit is many times higher than your average loss. That's the deciding factor!

Therefore, you should always be aware of the reaction of the market when you begin to increase your position. If the market confirms your assumption over and over again (for example, if it keeps rising on a long position) then you should continue buying. If the market does not do that by going sideways or even falling, it is clear that you should rather take a defensive wait-and-see stance. After all, you do not want to get a margin call from your broker.

I admit that I am an aggressive buyer once the market confirms my assumption and my first contracts are in profit. I cannot stress this issue enough. With this method, it's really about learning to massively step in, if you're right. The market itself is your best provider of feedback. I hope that I have clarified what this is all about, with my examples in this book. Classic risk management does not apply here. You calculate your risk by first testing the water and then stepping in with a small position.

Should one work with stop buy orders as soon as the market reaches a certain level? If you like to work with stop buy orders, then do it that way. The fact is that every speculation is different and each has its own dynamics. Sometimes nothing happens for weeks, and then the market shoots up in a few days, as if there is no tomorrow. In such situations, of course, you should have the courage to buy more contracts aggressively, within a few hours.

On the other hand, there is also the case of a market gradually rising for weeks, like a flight of stairs. Then you have all the time in the world to build up your position bit by bit.

But do not expect it to work that way every time. In general, you will have to expect both ups and downs and reversals, so depending on how many contracts you have already purchased, the fluctuations in your profit-loss indicator can be significant. This is an inherent component of this strategy and you must be able to bear it.

This strategy is more of an art than a science. There is no rule that says you should buy a futures contract for every new 100 points gain, for example, if you are long in the Dow Jones future. If you feel comfortable with this approach, you should do it that way. But you should know that the Dow can easily correct by 1,000 points in one day (as of 2019).

Every trader is different and each has his own comfort zone. Mostly, I assume a wait-and-see attitude. At the start of the movement, I tend to buy a few contracts. If the market continues to go up and confirms my assumption, I keep on buying. In the last phase, if the chart rises like a rocket, I usually buy again, aggressively. As the examples have shown, you have to be aware that the biggest gain is often made in this exaggeration phase.

Therefore, there can be no static algorithm for building positions in a trend market. Every trend or exaggeration is different, and it is the trader's job to respond appropriately. I wish I could offer you a static model of how you should buy (or sell if you go short). Unfortunately, I have none. Of course, if you have little or no experience with this strategy, I recommend that you take a more conservative approach first and do not expand your position too much. But maybe that does not suit your nature. Maybe you want to go to the limit, just as I did with my silver trade. There is nothing wrong with that. I do not remember exactly how many contracts I bought at the end of that trade.. Somewhere between 20 and 30, I think. You see, this is not for the faint hearted. But neither is it is for speculators like Soros and Co. And by the way, not even for an "investor" like Warren Buffet. Just think of his famous Coca Cola position, where he invested a good 30% of his capital. Investors like Buffet and Soros are not cautious and do not spread their investments into many assets, in order to "minimize the risks." Those guys did not get rich because they were cautious and conservative. On the contrary. They became rich, because they realized that you have to get in big if there is an excellent chance. And with big, I mean really big. You become rich through concentration. Not through diversification.

Chapter 17
Speculation is easier than day trading

It must be clear, that the usual risk management methods are ineffective for this type of speculation. Since you are pushing it to the limit, I recommend that you provide a certain amount of money, that you should write off from the beginning, for each speculation. In other words, you have to assume that you might lose your money, either because the market you invest in is not going in the direction you were hoping for, or because your timing was bad.

Of course, I try to minimize this risk by going in with just a small test position at first. However, it could happen that an unexpected reversal puts your position out of the market, even though it had already risen considerably and the whole thing looked good at first. That was the case with my ruble speculation, where I almost dropped out. Speculating on the stock market remains unpredictable and a trend can turn around completely any time. That's why I recommend taking calculated risks and writing off the money from the outset.

Try to see it like this. Is it bad if you lose USD 2,000 three times in a row – that's USD 6,000 in total – and then make USD 30,000 on your fourth attempt?

That would end up being an excellent result of USD 24,000 net profit. If you use this method, you have to look at it this way. This certainly does not suit risk-averse individuals. But, I did not write the book for those people.

I also claim that it is much easier to earn USD 24,000 with four targeted speculations (of which three go wrong) than trying to earn that kind of money by doing day trading, in which you risk USD 100 or USD 200 with every trade. That's a lot harder, believe me, I've been trying to do it for years.

The method of targeted speculation with levered instruments is not only simpler, it is also much more effective, whatever day traders may tell you.

Does that mean that you should not day trade anymore, and that, from now on, you should try to earn your money with a few targeted trades? No, that is not what I mean, because there are definitely times, at which you can do very well with day trading or scalping. If you enjoy it and you are doing well, carry on doing it. I'm just pointing out that there are times when day trading and scalping do not work so well. Then you should at least have an alternative method.

That may be the type of targeted speculation I am talking about here, or maybe an automatic trading system. It does not matter. What is important, is that you have an alternative when things are not going that well.

Chapter 18

A separate account for each speculation

I have one more recommendation if you want to use this method. Open a new account with another broker for each new speculation. Yes, you read correctly. Open an account specifically for each speculation, so, solely for this specific speculation. Nowadays, it is no longer difficult to open an account with a broker in just an hour.

So when I plan to build a position in a particular market, I choose the *right* broker, the broker I can best achieve my goals with. It is important to me that I have not previously traded on this account (i.e. no loss trades). Why is that important to me? Without feeling superstitious, I consider every new speculation as a kind of small business, which I open for a limited time and then close again. And most importantly, if my new business was successful, I withdraw the entire profit, including the initial capital, from the account and close the account!

Each new account is therefore intended for a specific trade, which I intend to do. And *only* for this trade.

So I do not try to use the account for other small sideline trades. Quite the opposite. I take the money out of the speculative cycle and I put it in a normal checking account. This way, the profit is definitely out of the risk zone. I can then do something nice with it or invest it, for example, by buying an apartment that I can rent out, or I could make another investment, such as buying physical gold.

This drastic measure will discipline you. You only have one shot, so to speak. If you fail on your first try, get out and come back another time and trade another market. Do not make the mistake that I made, of entering the same market several times. Choose something else. Because if you have burned your fingers in a certain market, you cannot see it with fresh eyes. You are, so to speak, prejudiced. I hope you can see that.

One could understand this "one trade per account method" as a kind of guerrilla tactic. You lie in wait (for a long time), you attack in optimal conditions, and then you literally get out, and cover your tracks. You do not like the sound of it? Just give it a try and you'll see how it feels.

Incidentally, I hope that you have not overlooked the fact *that I lie in wait for a <u>long</u> time*. I do the opposite of what most traders who trade permanently or have positions all the time do. Sorry, I have become a pretty minimalist trader. When people ask what I'm doing, I usually say "<u>nothing</u>." And, that's usually the case. Mostly, I do not do anything. That means, I do not spread my concentration too thin, with suboptimal trades that do not really advance my financial existence.

You just made three trades and you have USD 1,000 more in your account. Congratulations. But does this money really help you financially? Can you buy a house or make a significant investment with this money? I think that is unlikely. Why should one deal with such trades? However, if you are able to earn USD 100,000 with a single trade, then this money will really help you (for most people, anyway). And that's the point. Any trade that does not take you to a new financial level is not worth considering at all. If you go the stock exchange, then it should be worth it. Old master Kostolany used to say: If it's pork, it must be oozing!

And this new financial level might be different for everyone. For some, this may be USD 10,000, for somebody else it could be USD 100,000 or even a million. It does not matter. The key is that YOU get ahead. And, to do so, optimal preparation is necessary. In other words, with this method, you will have to morph from a hyperactive trader into a keen observer.

Chapter 19
With which financial instruments should I trade?

You need to be aware, that with a small trading account, you cannot play the full range of possible financial instruments. So do not think about imitating John Paulson, who made USD 3.7 billion in 2007 with a bet against the pompous American real estate market. He did that by buying credit default swaps (CDS). These instruments are not available to you as a retail investor. Incidentally, the whole thing about Paulson's trade was not really kosher. These instruments had been specially developed for him, so that he could bet against the banks that had issued them for him...

Of course, every retail investor can speculate with government bonds and currencies, and nobody can forbid that you short sell Ukrainian stocks if that country gets into trouble again.

Depending on which investment idea is involved, I will, as already mentioned, create the account with which I can best (and most cost-effectively) implement this idea.

Of course, if you choose **futures** for your speculation, you need a specialized (and inexpensive) futures broker. Above all, you should look at the amount of the overnight margins for your idea. If they are too high, you may need too much capital to even start. Compare several brokers. You will be amazed at the differences. The cheapest are usually American futures brokers, because they are often members of the CME themselves, which gives them very different terms.

If futures are too expensive for you, you can try a financial construct that is basically nothing more than a derivative on futures. This refers to **CFDs** or Contracts for Difference. You can open a CFD account with USD 1,000 or less. Unfortunately American citizens are not allowed to open a CFD account. Therefore, US citizens should have a look at **options** as a cheaper alternative to futures. I think options are an excellent instrument to trade the way I am referring to here.

CFD traders, in particular, should pay attention to the financing costs of these instruments, and ask the broker beforehand, what it would cost you to keep 10 CFDs in a given market for 3 months. Some brokers do not impose any financing costs on CFDs on futures, unlike with CFDs on stocks. This sometimes varies from broker to broker. I did my silver trade in 2007 - 2008 with CFDs. In the beginning, I started with mini-contracts, but as my position grew, I was able to buy the big contract, which eventually led to the big gain. However, after three months, I had over 1,000 euros in financing costs with this position. Had I known that I was going to stay in this trade for so long, I would surely have chosen another (cheaper) broker. I hope you understand better now, why I think it makes sense to open a separate account for each specific speculation idea.

Another instrument that can be used to speculate on developments in the markets, are **ETFs**. The big offer available in those instruments is now so confusing that you should think carefully about where you open an account. There is also the possibility of leverage, thanks to the so-called leveraged ETFs (often triple). So you can, for example, buy a triple leveraged ETF on silver.

Critics of ETFs (rightly) argue the problem of so-called *path dependence*. This phenomenon occurs especially in sideways movements or minor corrections in a trend. As long as the market moves in the desired direction, the return is even slightly stronger than the original leverage. If it goes the other way, the ETF usually underperforms. This disadvantage has an impact on long-term exposure to a market, which is why I believe leveraged ETFs are not suitable for long-term investors. For speculators who enter the market in the medium term (1 to 3 months) and, above all, rely on a strong move in the underlying, I think it can even be an excellent instrument.

Probably the easiest and most flexible tool for a retail investor are the **forex markets**. Here you can even participate with very small amounts (under USD 1,000). And maybe the forex market is also the best starting point for this strategy. However, here, one should also note the amount of the financing costs, which are better known under the term "swaps". Swaps are interest rates incurred on borrowing (which is usually a forex position). Interest rates of 5% may well occur. Therefore, when choosing a forex broker you should pay less attention to spreads and levels of leverage than swaps. An in-depth comparison of brokers in this regard can mean that you may save several thousand dollars. This is particularly true when dealing with exotic currencies, i.e. currencies that are not part of the classic Big 7 (EUR, USD, GBP, CHF, CAD, AUD, NZD). These are, for example, currency pairs like USD/RUB, USD/MXN or EUR/TRY. The swaps in these currencies can accumulate significantly if you invest in one of them for months.

Chapter 20

Maximum risk and Margin Call

If you decide to trade with professional instruments, such as futures and options, you should know that from the point of view of risk management, you are considered as a "professional partner". <u>Futures and options transactions are generally subject to an obligation to make additional contributions.</u> If the losses from your positions exceed the margin coverage, you will receive a margin call from your broker. This means that money has to be topped up, otherwise the position will be closed.

If you do not like the idea that, theoretically, you can lose more than you have available, you may want to refrain from trading these instruments. But when talking to brokers, this occurs relatively rarely in practice. Usually, the margin calls are already threat enough to a trader to reduce the position or close it completely if necessary. Nevertheless, as a trader, you should be aware that the requirement for additional funding exists. If possible, you should never let it get that far. Several brokers I've talked to about the issue have assured me that in the rare cases in which this happened, they were always able to reach an agreement with the trader.

By contrast, if you trade derivative instruments, such as CFDS or Forex, you are usually on the safe side, at least within the EU. Because of the strict regulation of the European supervisory authority ESMA, which has been in force since the beginning of August 2018, the high leverage for private investors has been severely limited. Previously, leverages of 100 to 500 were common, but they are now limited to a maximum of the factor 30. Depending on the underlying value, they are even lower – with stocks they are about five, at most. Traders are therefore not obliged to make additional contributions, should the deposited security no longer be sufficient. The losses cannot exceed the invested capital.

If you want to guard against such an event, despite this rule, you can look for a broker who offers a <u>guaranteed stop-loss order</u>. Here, the broker guarantees the closing of the position exactly at the desired price. The broker therefore bears the risk and must pay the costs of deviations himself. In return, the trader usually pays a fee for this guarantee. The fee can also be collected by widening the spreads. You should therefore consider this charge as a kind of insurance premium. Talk to your broker and ask him if he offers guaranteed stop-loss orders, and what they cost.

Chapter 21
Keep your trades to yourself

As a speculator, you'll have to be prepared to do unpopular things if you want to make serious money, or if you want to move your account forward. And not everyone is going to like what you are doing. I would like to give you some advice, as a trader friend. If possible, <u>do not talk to anyone about your trades</u>. Open an account with a broker and do your transactions. Do not talk about it. Not even to your friends, and certainly not to your family. The reason is simple. Hardly anyone will understand what you are doing. I do not mean understanding in the moral sense, but technically speaking. For example, if you do a short sale, no one will understand it, even if you do your best to explain it to them. If you buy USD/RUB, technically speaking, you are long US dollars, short Russian rubles. Try explaining that to your grandmother. If she has never done it herself, she will not understand.

Look at the stock market reports on the news. They hardly ever report on what really matters. The media craves sensation, panic or drama, or they wag their moral index finger at you. Rarely do they report facts about what is really happening. So do not be surprised when your friends, acquaintances or family babble about what the media presents them with. And do not expect anyone to show understanding for your "new occupation". That is something you will rarely get.

Regarding the impact and the task of the financial markets, the general public is stupid. It is deliberately kept stupid. That might not appeal to you, but it is a fact. There are countries where trading is a little less stigmatized. This is the case, for example, in the USA. Unlike in Europe, people there are happy when **you** are successful. But I can assure you that this is much less the case in most other countries. Scolding the evil speculators is a simple way to blow off steam on something you do not understand.

But there is a much more important reason why you should keep your trades to yourself. If you start talking about your plans or even about ongoing positions with your fellow human beings, they will respond in some way. The best thing that could happen to you would be indifference, because that harms you least. But imagine if I had told an acquaintance that I was speculating against the ruble, maybe even in the days when everyone could see on TV, how people in Russia were queuing up outside the exchange office to get rid of their rubles. Do you think I would have made friends like that? Of course not. That could incite very moral thinking people against you. You would have to begin defending yourself, or you might even have to begin justifying yourself. And that's the last thing you should do if you're in the middle of a speculation. These conversations or discussions with people who have no idea about the matter will only confuse you in the end. Worse still, it could cause you to begin to doubt the one thing with which you might have financial success.

Now, there are quite a few traders who solve their need for communication by visiting so-called like-minded people. Either they belong to a stock club or they search the internet for forums or chat rooms, in which they can discuss their trades to their heart's content. I admit that I did this in my beginners' years too (I started in 2001). At that time, the trading forums were something new. In fact, at the time you were sometimes able to meet a successful trader who was willing to share his experience with you.

However, I can tell you from my own experience, that the vast majority of successful traders I know have long since withdrawn from these chats and stock market forums. If you really have something sensible to say on the subject and you are constantly being attacked by some dummies, what do you do? Right!

You take your hat and disappear forever. I do not want to rule out that there are no idealists who still visit these haunts, but sometimes the level in the pub around the corner is a haven of philosophy and human knowledge, compared to what you can experience in stock market chats. I have long since said goodbye to that (over 10 years ago). I would rather recommend telling your mother-in-law about your stock market engagements, than that you set foot in one of these internet chats, where no one has to answer personally and almost everyone participates under a pseudonym (or several pseudonyms). So do not do it. The reason is the same as with your family or friends. The chance of these people clouding your unbiased view of the markets is quite large. Remember the attitude of Jesse Livermore, who even locked himself in a room, so he could not hear the chatter of the other speculators. I never made money while I was in these forums. On the contrary.

And that brings me to my real concern. No matter what you do in life, whether you're starting a business or starting a trading business, <u>you'll have to do it alone</u>. You 'll have to go this goddamn way alone. And you cannot allow anyone to interfere with it in any way, least of all, your mother-in-law and certainly not some idiot on the internet, who hides his true identity from you. I cannot stress this enough. You will only be successful when you start to become an independent trader personality. Now everyone knows that there are only a few of them. The vast majority of people play the game safely and wander on much-traveled paths. There is nothing wrong with that. If you like, I can also say it esoterically for those who believe in it: if you have chosen to push a quiet ball for this incarnation, then look for a safe government job. Find something in the administration. Or how about a job at the tax office?

But if you want success, real success, <u>then you will have to do something unusual.</u> You will have to do things that those who prefer to push a quiet ball do not want, and therefore reject. I hope you now understand why it is better to keep your financial affairs to yourself.

Chapter 22
On the way to the first million

One million dollars is certainly a high target, especially for someone who has just over a few thousand dollars available to speculate with. However, I hope that, with the examples I have shown you in this book, it will be possible to make significant profits on the stock market with small sums, no matter what some skeptics say. If I can do it, so can you.

But even though duplication and multiplication in small accounts are quite feasible, they are not so easy to achieve for larger amounts – but not impossible either. As you know, you only need to double 10 times to make a million from 1,000. It is hopefully clear to the reader that the step from 1,000 to 2,000 is quite different than the jump from 250,000 to 500,000, although mathematically it is the same principle.

Everyone who is active on the stock market should be able to get over the loss of USD 1,000. But can you afford to lose USD 250,000?

I'm well aware that there are traders who have suffered such losses (and even much more). At the end of this book, I would like to emphasize once again, that you should not let it come to that, with the method presented here.

The idea of this method is <u>to take calculated risks</u>. This minimizes the risk of a total loss of the available capital. You should become a specialist in speculation, achieving the maximum with minimal effort. Precisely for that reason, I recommend that you deduct the majority of your profits from the brokerage account and withdraw them from the speculative cycle. If you ever make USD 30,000 profit with a speculation, then withdraw at least USD 20,000 from the brokerage account. For the method presented here, by no means do you need USD 30,000 to speculate. On the contrary. I recommend keeping these totals small (this measure will teach you discipline).

If at first glance, this method could be classified as "high risk", but this measure makes it less risky than initially suspected. The highest risk is in the beginning, when the available capital is still small. The further you progress, the less risky it will be if you consistently enter the market with just a small test position at first, and only buy more when you already have book profits.

Of course, you can risk a little more if you can call the first USD 100,000 your own. But since, for most speculation, usually no more than a few thousand dollars margin are required, there is no reason to leave USD 50,000 in your brokerage account. Be smart and minimize your initial risk as much as you can.

Maybe it will go a bit slower until you reach your first million, but you will reach your destination without undue stress. Maybe you are able to make profits of USD 100,000 a few times, or the money will trickle in gradually in USD 40,000 snacks. No matter how you do it, you should make sure that you put away most of your profits, and never risk them again.

This measure is just the opposite of what most traders do. They leave their profits in the brokerage account, so they can trade more and more contracts. For these traders, therefore, the bigger the account gets, the more the risk increases. I try to do the opposite. The further you progress, the more capital you should always draw from the speculative cycle. Remember, trading profits are not really yours, unless you have completely withdrawn them from the brokerage account, and preferably locked them away or invested them conservatively.

That way, you will have the highest risk at the beginning of your career as a speculator, and not at the end. Be smart. You can always speculate, but lost investment capital never comes back.

It is important to clearly understand the difference between a speculator and an investor. They have different goals, and therefore use different methods. The goal of a speculator should be to progress financially, as quickly and efficiently as possible. In this book, I have tried to portray how that is done.

The goal and task of an investor is a completely different one. An investor <u>already has capital</u>. His primary objective is to protect existing assets and to maintain purchasing power through a realistic and risk-free return.

I hope you realize that these are two completely different goals. The ultimate goal of your endeavor is not to have the largest possible amount of money in your brokerage account, but <u>financial freedom</u>. We will look at how to achieve this in the next chapter.

Chapter 23

The Final Goal: Financial Freedom

Even if the first million seems like quite a distant goal to many, it is not out of reach. The method presented here can be regarded as an important step on the way to this goal, it need not be the only one. By the way, I consider the nominal sum of one million dollars more like a symbolic goal. As strange as this may seem to non-wealthy readers, a million on the bank today is more of a problem than a solution. The times when such a sum would give you a yearly risk-free interest yield of 5 or 6% are long gone. And those countries with higher interest rates do not necessarily offer a solution either, because the compounding will be eaten up by the inflation or alternatively, the fraudulent state will seize the capital on a flimsy justification, as happened to a friend of mine who had parked a considerable sum in a Ukrainian account.

In other words, current interest rates are forcing anyone with some money to become an investor, whether they want to or not.

The method presented here aims to make quick financial progress. It's undoubtedly an unorthodox method, but trust me, it's being used by more traders than you'd expect. Many a trader, who perhaps outwardly sells a particular system with strict risk management, secretly does exactly what I'm talking about here, without ever saying a word about it in public.

My only goal with this book has been to present a way with which you, as a trader, can quickly achieve your financial goals. Of course you can also do it with traditional methods, such as day trading or swing trading. These methods are and will remain valid. But they demand an unshakeable discipline from the trader, that most of us – let's be honest – do not have. That's the reason why the number of traders who fail with these strategies is so large.

The method presented here assumes that most of us are not disciplined traders, but ordinary people who make mistakes every now and then.

But if, as suggested here, you bet on specific events or strong stock market trends, you only need to be right a few times. But then, when you are right, you should have the courage to step in big. Many traders, like Jesse Livermore, did it this way, gradually working their way up from humble beginnings.

Of course, you will not succeed with every speculation. Sometimes your position will barely earn you any money. Sometimes maybe only a few thousand dollars. Do not feel discouraged. If you stick to this idea, you will one day find the market in which you can make USD 100,000 or even more.

If you skim off USD 70,000 of this money, you can buy a house or another asset. Invest this money into something you will still benefit from in ten years' time. Preferably buy an asset that flushes money into your pocket monthly. The latest Tesla, for example, does not fall into this category. This toy will pull money out of your pocket and will be worth less month by month.

And that brings us to the important difference between an asset and a liability. An asset regularly flushes money into your pockets. A liability, on the other hand, costs you money. I owe this clear distinction to the books of Robert Kiyosaki. If you do not know them yet, I recommend you to buy them now.

Another way to generate monthly cash flow is to build a dividend portfolio with your earnings. This is one way to profit from your profits over decades. It's really fun if you have something like that, believe me. You then own a cash machine that will bring you money every month, without you having to do anything big for it.

In other words, my recommendation is that you do not go from speculation to speculation until you finally have this million in your bank account. It may sound great to say: I am a millionaire. But this title does not mean much in times of zero interest rates.

And you may be surprised when I say now: <u>it is even not desirable to have one million on the bank.</u>

I want to explain this with a nice story. A friend of mine founded a company that he wanted to sell one day. And he also had enough interested buyers. He figured out he could get four million dollars for his business. Many would say: great, now he can really cash in, and live from the fruits of his labor. Not even close. My friend kept delaying the sale of his company. "Why?" I asked him when I met him again. It turned out he was really scared of the sale. Of course there were various reasons. But one of the most important was that he felt safe as long as his business belonged to him, and he was able to pay himself a (generous) executive salary month after month. Because, if he sold the business he would no longer have a salary. "Yes, but you could have four million in the bank," I countered. "Sure," he answered, "only this money will bring me hardly anything. What am I going to live on? "

This story may seem absurd to some readers, because they believe that anyone who has that kind of money in the bank will no longer have financial problems. Unfortunately, the opposite is true. If you have a million or even more in the bank, then you actually have a problem, as absurd as it may seem to less wealthy individuals. This "million in the bank" is nothing but a petty bourgeois dream. This dream is also the reason why so many people play the lottery. And it's also why so many lottery millionaires lose everything after a while.

This million brings you hardly anything today. My friend knew that. Unfortunately, during his entrepreneurial life, he failed to invest the money he earned into assets that would have earned him a monthly cash flow (that is, a passive income). He had hardly any real estate. He had speculated a little with stocks and mostly lost. Unfortunately, the word "dividend" was alien to him.

Rather than hoarding a million on the bank or even in a trading account, it's important to learn how to invest that money properly. In other words, in addition to your speculator career, <u>you should also silently build up an investor's career.</u>

Because that's what the really wealthy have always done. They always have money, no matter what happens, because they (or their ancestors) have invested capital over and over again in assets: land, real estate, company holdings, licenses, lease income, dividends.

And when the cash flow for these assets began to exceed the sum of their monthly expenses, they used that free cash to buy even more assets that brought them even more money. In the so-called "old money families" this was done from generation to generation.

And that's exactly how you should do it, in my opinion. You should not use your occasional stock market successes to build up an ever-growing account, with which you may splurge with your friends. No, do it right from the start. Learn to siphon off most of your profits and invest them in long-term assets. Do not wait until you have four million in your account, because then you might have the same problem as my entrepreneur friend. Or the same problem as the lottery millionaires, who disappear after a while.

Therefore, in my eyes, the goal of "one million in the bank" is a decoy. Such a sum may inspire your imagination. It is however better if you increase your financial IQ right from the start and learn how to invest in the long term, so that you can still benefit from this money decades after your stock market successes. It is possible. But only if you start right from the beginning.

So take the most of your profits out, and lock it away. With the rest, you can continue to speculate and hunt for lucrative opportunities. I wish you success!

Addendum 1: Past financial crises

The history of the financial world is rich in financial crises. As I said, whatever is dangerous or ruinous to some, may represent an opportunity for others. That has always been the case. If you want to become wealthy with stock market speculation, you are well advised to study past financial crises. Here is a list which is certainly not complete. Study these crises! You will then be better equipped to recognize future ones. In addition to the crises, you will also find the possible speculations that you could have traded successfully.

1973: Oil Crisis, long Oil, short Stocks

1973: Banking Crisis United Kingdom: short British Equities

1983: Bank Crisis Israel, short Israeli Stocks

1986 - 1991: Japanese Bubble Industry: short Nikkei, long Yen

1994 - 1995: Tequila Crisis Mexico: short Mexican Peso

1997 - 1998: Asian Crisis, short Indonesian Rupiah, Thai Baht, South Korean Won

1999: Brazil Crisis, short Brazilian Real

1998 - 1999: Russia crisis, short Russian ruble

2001: Turkish crisis: short lira, short shares

2001 - 2002: Argentina Crisis, short Argentine Peso

2000: Dotcom Crisis, short Nasdaq

2007 - 2008: Subprime Crisis, long Gold Silver, short Stocks

2008: Iceland Crisis, short Icelandic Krona

2007 - 2008: Spanish Real Estate Crisis, Short IBEX (Spanish Equities)

2010: Greek sovereign debt crisis, short ATHEX (Greek equities)

2010: Spanish savings bank crisis, short Spanish stocks

2010: Euro crisis, short Euro

2014: Russian financial crisis, short Ruble

2018: Turkish Financial Crisis, short Lira, short Turkish Stocks

As you can see, there is no shortage of crises. Almost every year there is a fire somewhere, from which you can benefit as a speculator.

Incidentally, there are not many different types of crises. Here is a list of the most important types:

- banking crises
- currency crises
- speculative bubbles
- sovereign debt crises (a state cannot repay its debt)
- economic stagnation and recessions

If you want to deepen your knowledge of financial crises, I can recommend the following books:

- Barry Eichengreen: Hall of Mirrors: The Great Depression, the Great Recession, and the Uses- and Misuses-of History, Oxford University Press 2016
- Ray Dalio: Big Debt Crises, Bridgewater 2018
- Carmen M. Reinhart, Kenneth S. Rogoff: This Time Is Different: Eight Centuries of Financial Folly, Princeton University Press 2009
- Robert Z. Aliber, Charles P. Kindleberger: Manias, Panics, and Crashes: A History of Financial Crises, Palgrave Macmillan 2017

Addendum 2: Useful websites

Good overview charts: https://finviz.com

Investment calculator: https://www.calculator.net/investment-calculator.html

Long-term charts: https://www.barchart.com/futures/long-term-trends?viewName=chart

https://www.macrotrends.net/

Glossary

AEX: Stock index of the Netherlands, which is calculated on Euronext Amsterdam

Averaging down: Process of buying additional shares of a stock at lower prices than the original purchase price. This lowers the average price an investor pays for the whole position

Bond: A bond, also known as a fixed-income security, is an interest-bearing security

Book profit: Difference between the purchase price and the current price. This profit initially exists only on paper. Only when the stock is sold, can it be realized

Bovespa: (Índice Bovespa, abbreviated Ibovespa) leading stock index in Brazil. It consists of 71 companies

Break Even: Point at which there is neither profit nor loss

Brexit: The withdrawal of the United Kingdom from the European Union

Broker: A financial service provider responsible for executing securities orders from investors

CAC 40: French benchmark index of the 40 leading French companies listed on the Paris Stock Exchange

Candlestick: Representation of price changes based on a Japanese analysis technique

Cash Flow: The difference in revenue and expenditure over a period of time

CFD: Payment agreement, the value of which is the difference between the prices of the underlying value, such as a share or currency, at the time of purchase and sale of the CFD

CME: The US-based CME Group is one of the world's largest option exchanges and the world's largest derivatives exchange, based in Chicago, Illinois

Commissions: costs incurred on the purchase and sale of securities

Credit Default Swaps: (CDS) Credit derivative in which default risks of loans are traded

Day trading: describes short-term speculative trading in securities. Positions are opened and closed within the same trading day

Dividend: part of the profit that a public company distributes to its shareholders

Dow Jones: The oldest surviving stock index in the US, today comprising 30 of the largest US companies

Doji: Frequently occurring pattern in a candlestick chart. It is characterized in that it has a short length, which means a small trading margin, with the opening and closing price being almost the same

Downgrading: Downgrade of a security

Entry Strategy: A strategy that determines the entry into a market

ESMA: European Securities and Markets Authority

ETF: Exchange Traded Funds

Euro crisis: describes a complex crisis of the European Monetary Union from the year 2010

Exit strategy: A strategy that determines the exit from a market

EUR/CHF: Currency ratio between the Euro and the Swiss franc

EUR/TRY: Currency ratio between the Euro and the Turkish Lira

European Exchange Rate Mechanism: a form of monetary cooperation between the countries of the European Community, from March 13, 1979 to December 31, 1998

Fait accompli: A French term that is often used to describe an action that is completed before those affected can question or reverse it

Financial Crisis: Global Banking and Financial Crisis as Part of the Global Economic Crisis as of 2007

Flat: Flat position

Francogeddon: On January 15, 2015, the Swiss National Bank lifted the minimum euro exchange rate of 1.20 without warning. The Swiss franc increased in price by almost 20 percent

Forex: Forex Exchange Market, International Currency Market

Forwards: Non-exchange-traded, unconditional forward transactions

Futures: Standardized contract for the purchase or sale of a certain quantity of a commodity, at a fixed price, on a given date

Gap: price gap between two trading days

Global macro: Investment strategy based on the interpretation and forecasting of major events related to economies, history and international relations.

Hedging: Method of securing a transaction against financial risks, such as price fluctuations

Heikin Ashi Chart: Japanese: "balancing on one foot". Japanese representation of price changes

Hit rate: The hit rate describes the ratio of winning trades to losing trades

Initial Margin: Amount of collateral required to open a position

Interest rate: Fixed by a central bank within the framework of its monetary policy, based upon which it concludes transactions with its affiliated banks

Leverage effect: The use of borrowed capital increases the return on the use of one's own capital

Lira Crisis: The Turkish Currency and Debt Crisis 2018

Long: Being Long means buying and holding securities holdings

Margin: Secured position for exchange transactions by depositing a certain pledge

Market Efficiency Hypothesis: According to this theory, financial markets are efficient insofar as existing information is already priced in, and thus no market participant is able to achieve above-average profits through technical analysis, fundamental analysis, insider trading or otherwise

Money management: Money management is a value preservation strategy that aims to manage the risk of a portfolio of securities by sizing each trade position

Nymex: The New York Mercantile Exchange (NYMEX) is the world's largest commodity futures exchange, based in New York

Option: Indicates a right to buy or sell a particular item at a later date, at an agreed price

Path dependence: Inverse effect, which applies from closing price to closing price. If the period becomes longer, deviations occur

Pip: Percentage in point, smallest change in the price in forex trading

Pyramiding: In stock trading, refers to the gradual establishment or reduction of positions

Quarterly earnings: Report of a stock corporation at the end of a quarter

Range: Price range in which a value is traded in one phase (one day, one week, several months)

Resistance: Price level, where more sellers emerge, than buyers

Reversal: Reversing a price trend within a trading day

Risk Management: Includes all measures for the systematic detection, analysis, assessment, monitoring and control of risks

Risk Reward Ratio (RRR): Serves as an indicator of the usefulness of a speculation. It is calculated by dividing the expected profitability by the largest possible loss

Scalping: Trading technique in which the trader tries to trade minimal movements in the market

Short position: a trader is short when he sells a position that he doesn't own (short sale)

SNB: Swiss National Bank

S&P 500 (Standard & Poor's 500): Stock index comprising the shares of 500 of the largest US listed companies

Spread: The spread between bid and ask prices

Stock index: Indicator of the performance of the stock market as a whole, or of individual stock groups (e.g. Dow Jones)

Stop Buy Order: An order to buy or sell securities, which will only be executed when the price reaches a certain price level

Stop Loss Order: A sell order that is best executed when a specific price is reached

Stop Management: Active management of stop orders during a trade

Swing trading: A trading strategy in which a security is held for between one and several days, in order to take advantage of price changes or fluctuations

Subprime crisis: Refers to a global banking and financial crisis as part of the global economic crisis as of 2007

Take Profit Order: Automated stock market order, triggered when a predetermined price target has been reached

Target price: Stock market price that a security should achieve, on the basis of an analysis

Tick: Smallest price change on a futures market

Trailing-Stop: Automatic stop-loss order

Trend Following: Trading strategy that focuses on following a trend that has been identified

Ukraine crisis: Political, at times armed conflict over the Crimean Peninsula

USD/CAD: Currency ratio between the US Dollar and the Canadian Dollar

USD/RUB: Currency ratio between the US Dollar and the Russian Ruble

Volatility: Standard deviation. Indicates how much a price fluctuates

Other Books by Heikin Ashi Trader

How to Scalp the Mini DAX Future?

Thanks to the introduction of the Mini-DAX futures (FDXM) private traders with smaller accounts are afforded the opportunity to scalp the German DAX Index to professional terms. Unlike most other trading instruments, Futures are the most transparent and effective way to make money in the financial markets.

Scalpers have infinitely more trading opportunities than position traders or day traders, which constitutes the real strength of this trading style. A scalper may therefore manage his capital much more effectively than all other market participants and thus achieve much greater returns than would otherwise be the case.

The Heikin Ashi Trader shows in this book how to successfully scalp this new future on the DAX. You will learn how to enter the market, how to manage your position and at which point you should back out. In addition, the book contains a wealth of tips and tools to make your trading even more effective and precise.

Table of Contents

1. The EUREX Introduces the Mini DAX Future
2. The German DAX, a Popular Market for International Traders
3. Advantages of Future Trading
4. The Heikin-Ashi Chart
5. What Is Scalping?
6. What is the Advantage of Being a Scalper?
7. Basic Setup of Heikin Ashi Scalping
8. Entry Strategies
9. Are Re-Entries Sensible?

10. Exit Strategies

11. Are Multiple Targets Sensible?

12. When You Should Scalp the Mini-DAX-Future (and When Not)

13. Useful Tools for Scalpers

    A. Placing Orders

    B. Open and Close Orders

    C. Managing Open Orders

    D. The Trailing Stop as a Profit Maximization Tool

14. Various Stop-Orders

    A. The Fix Stop

    B. The Trailing Stop

    C. The Linear Stop

    D. The Time Stop

    E. The Parabolic Stop

    F. Link Stop Orders

    G. Multiple Stops and Multiple Targets

15. On the Stock Exchange Money Is Made with Exit Strategies!

16. Further Development of Market Analysis

    A. Key Price Levels

    B. Live Statistics

Epilogu

Glossary

More Books by Heikin Ashi Trader

About the Author

How to Trade a Range

Trade the Most Interesting Market in the World

Financial markets are predominantly trading in trendless zones, which traders call trading ranges or sideways markets. It then appears that they earn money when a market is in a trend and they should avoid trendless markets, because here there is nothing to write home about.

Despite this apparent finding, most short-term trading strategies rely on the trend-following model, although it is demonstrably difficult to implement. Most traders are more or less looking for a bigger move. The experience shows, however, that trading „moves" or „trends" is not that easy. Either the trader recognizes the trend too late, or the movement offers hardly any opportunities to enter.

There is, however, a specialized group of traders who do not care about trends. They do exactly the opposite. They trade when the market is in a range. This book describes the methods and tactics of these traders. It is not about how to identify a range and then to trade the outbreak from it, but how to trade the range itself.

Table of Contents

1. Introduction to Range Trading

2. What Is a Range Market?

3. Look to the Left!

4. How Do I Draw Proper Support and Resistance Lines?

5. In Which Markets Can You Operate Range Trading?

6. How to Trade a Range in Practice?

7. Where Should I Place the Stop?

8. Questions of Trade Management

    A. Should You Close the Trade Before the Weekend?

    B. Should You Use Trailing Stops in Range Trading?

    C. What Should You Do if the Trade Goes "Nowhere"?

    D. Should I Push the Stop Closer to the Market?

9. Examples of Range Markets

   A. Trading Ranges in the Foreign Exchange Market

   B. Deeper Examination of a Sideways Period in the E-Mini

   C. Deeper Examination of a Sideways Period in the FDAX

10. Advanced Strategies

    A. Opportunistic Limits

    B. Fakeouts

11. Trend Channels (Channel Trading)

12. What Is Really Important

13. Range Trading for Day Traders and Scalpers

Glossary

Trade Against the Trend!

The brokerage industry usually recommends that new traders trade with the trend. But is trading this way profitable? It is said that if you go with the trend, the likelihood that you will win is higher. Unfortunately, experience shows that most traders cannot build a profitable business this way.

Old and experienced traders used to say: You have to buy when blood flows in the streets. That means that you should act against the trend. Actually, this saying is the expression of common sense itself. The question remains: Why do traders find it so hard to put this wisdom into practice?

The new book by Heikin Ashi Trader gives ideas and tips on how to recognize such countertrend signals in the stock market, since these are usually the best trading opportunities.

Table of Contents

Part 1: The Snapback Trading Strategy

Chapter 1: Trade when the mass is afraid

Chapter 2: Why I do not follow the trend

Chapter 3: Mean Reversion

Chapter 4: Risk Management

Chapter 5: How do I recognize extreme movements?

Chapter 6: Patience at the entry

Chapter 7: Does the stop really protect me from heavy losses?

Chapter 8: Trade Management

Chapter 9: Exit

Chapter 10: When do the best trading opportunities occur?

Chapter 11: Why you should study the economic calendar

Chapter 12: Which markets are suitable for the snapback strategy?

Part 2: Trading Examples

Chapter 1: Examples in the stock indices

Chapter 2: Examples in the currency markets (Forex)

Chapter 3: Examples in the stock markets

Chapter 4: Examples in the commodity markets

Glossary

About the Author

Heikin Ashi Trader is the pen name of a trader who has more than 18 years of experience in day trading futures and foreign exchange. He specializes in scalping and fast day trading. In addition to this, he has published multiple self-explanatory books on his trading activities. Popular topics are on: scalping, swing trading, money- and risk management.